# FINGERFOOD

## GREAT TASTES

D0943435

First published in 2010 by Bay Books, an imprint of Murdoch Books Pty Limited

Murdoch Books Australia
Pier 8/9
23 Hickson Road
Millers Point NSW 2000
Phone: +61 (0) 2 8220 2000
Fax: +61 (0) 2 8220 2558
www.murdochbooks.com.au

Murdoch Books UK Limited
Erico House, 6th Floor
93–99 Upper Richmond Road
Putney, London SW15 2TG
Phone: +44 (0) 20 8785 5995
Fax: +44 (0) 20 8785 5985
www.murdochbooks.co.uk

Chief Executive: Juliet Rogers
Publishing Director: Kay Scarlett
Publisher: Lynn Lewis
Senior Designer: Heather Menzies
Designer: Melanie Young
Production: Kita George
Index: Jo Rudd

© Text, design and photography copyright Murdoch Books 2010.
All rights reserved. No part of this publication may be reproduced, stored in a retrieval system or transmitted in any form or by any means, electronic, mechanical, photocopying, recording or otherwise, without the prior written permission of the publisher.

ISBN: 9781741966985

PRINTED IN CHINA

IMPORTANT: Those who might be at risk from the effects of salmonella poisoning (the elderly, pregnant women, young children and those suffering from immune deficiency diseases) should consult their doctor with any concerns about eating raw eggs.

OVEN GUIDE: You may find cooking times vary depending on the oven you are using. For fan-forced ovens, as a general rule, set the oven temperature to 20°C (35°F) lower than indicated in the recipe.

GREAT TASTES

# FINGERFOOD

More than 120 easy recipes for every day

bay books

# CONTENTS

# FINGERFOOD BASICS

If you're having a party, you want to make sure that you have just as much fun as your guests. Easy! Simply plan ahead so that you can relax on the day. All the fingerfood in this book was chosen for its suitability as party food. That's not to say that you can't serve some of the recipes as an entrée or for other occasions; it just means that people will find the food easy to eat while they're standing up. Most of the food items are small enough that your guests won't have to struggle with their food, plate, glass and serviette, with dignity the loser!

## What's the occasion?

If you are planning a party, your first decision should be what kind of party you want to have. Will it be casual, formal, simple or lavish? Will there be a sit-down dinner to follow or will it just be drinks and canapés? Will it last for a couple of hours or all night long?

## When and where?

Next, you will need to work out when and where to hold your party. Obviously, the time of year will have a big impact on the venue (for example, whether it is indoors or outdoors), but it will also affect the menu. People's eating habits change with the season: we tend to eat more filling food in the colder months and prefer lighter food when the temperature rises. So let the season be your guide when planning your menu.

The time of day will also influence your catering demands. You need to consider when your guests will have last eaten a full meal and whether they will be dining after the party. Guests who have come straight from work will generally have a hearty appetite, while those who are planning to eat after the party will be more likely to eat less.

## Your guests

Another factor to consider when planning your menu is your guests. It is not only the number of people you invite that is important, but also the type of people you are inviting. What food will they enjoy? A party of footballers fresh from a grand final match, for example, will probably not be satisfied with a few delicate bites. Use your discretion here; however, a good rule of thumb with a mixed crowd is to serve a couple of conservative canapés such as tarts and party pies, plus something bread-based (especially if you are serving alcohol), then to follow these with a selection of more innovative canapés. It's a good idea to include at least two vegetarian options for a mixed group.

## How much to serve?

One of the most important elements of party planning is making sure there is enough food to last duration of the party. Use the following rough guide as a starting point, then think about the other factors already mentioned to make your final selection. The recipes have serving sizes, so refer to them when planning.

For pre-dinner nibbles, serve about 3–5 pieces of food per person. For a two- or three-hour cocktail party, allow 3–5 pieces per hour for each person. For a full-length party, which generally lasts about four hours, a total of 12–15 pieces of fingerfood per person is a generous amount. You would normally taper off the food towards the end of the party. If your party lasts for longer than four hours, you should consider serving a light supper or meal at the end.

Nibbles such as nuts and chips are not included in this calculation, but they are very useful fillers at casual gatherings. Be aware that the more formal the gathering, the less people tend to eat. Friends will tuck in at a casual party, but are more restrained at a formal event.

It's a good idea to let your friends know what kind of occasion you are planning so that they don't come expecting an evening meal and leave ravenous after a few canapés. If you are planning a two-hour cocktail party, put start and finish times on the invitation; that way people will be expecting nibbles and won't be disappointed. If it is an all-evening affair, let them know you'll be providing the food equivalent to an evening meal.

*Timber foodpicks*

*Sugar cubes*

*Napkins*

*Sauce bowls*

## The canapés

Whatever the size or type of your party, don't forget to consider the limitations of your equipment, time and budget. A few platters of well-chosen ideas will create more impact and give you more freedom than attempting 20 different recipes. You can always add some ready-made snacks to round out your menu.

As a general rule, if you are having between 10 and 20 guests, provide about six different canapés and, for any more guests than that, offer 8–10 different types. When you pick them, try not to repeat main ingredients; for example, don't serve prawn dumplings as well as lemongrass prawns. When serving, start with a selection of cold canapés, then move onto the hot ones.

If guests are staying for the whole evening, you might want to provide one or two sweet canapés towards the end of the party to indicate that the party is ending.

## Being prepared

As well as trying to choose a balanced menu, be kind to yourself by picking some foods that can be prepared well ahead (even frozen), some that can be made a couple of days in advance and just one or two that need to be finished on the day. At the end of some of our recipes you will find a 'Note' that lets you know what can be done beforehand. Limit those to be made on the day to simple frying, baking or garnishing and make sure you have some help (either a friend or hospitality agency staff) doing the last-minute touches.

Write a detailed list of what you need to buy, what can be prepared in advance and when you should do it.

Make sure you have enough equipment to make, store and serve the canapés; particularly consider refrigeration, heating and frying requirements.

## Presentation

At a party, presentation is important to complement the food. Apart from normal platters and trays to serve food, you can use lacquered trays, steamer baskets lined with banana leaves, platters lined with vine leaves, or sushi mats and trays lined with napkins or coloured paper (change the paper when you replenish the tray).

And for the presentation of the food itself, there are sprigs of herbs, Chinese spoons and shot glasses. Whatever you choose, make sure that you have plenty of them—borrow from friends or hire from a catering agency, if necessary. If you know that space will be tight at the party, avoid large heavy platters that are hard to circulate.

When arranging the food, don't crowd it. Arrange one, or at the most two, kinds of canapés on a tray at a time. They look best placed in neat, evenly spaced rows on the diagonal. Lastly, don't forget to provide for the practicalities: somewhere for people to put discarded skewers, toothpicks or napkins. You'll be amazed what a difference a little planning makes to your enjoyment of the party!

## Equipment list

Fridge/freezer space

Baking trays

Toothpicks/cocktail sticks

Spoons and forks

Napkins

Coasters

Glasses or plastic cups

Plates

Platters and trays

Serving bowls (big/small)

Small tables

Bowls for discarded toothpicks

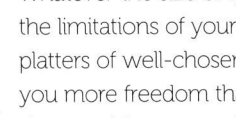

*Cocktail napkins*

*Cocktail olive fork*

*Toothpicks*

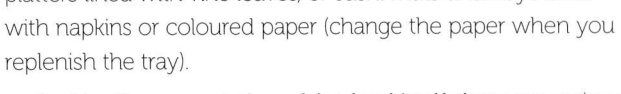

*Chinese soup spoons*

# NIBBLES

# HONEY-ROASTED PEANUTS

**MAKES 475 G (1 LB 2 OZ/2½ CUPS)**

350 g (12 oz/2 cups) raw shelled
  peanuts

175 g (6 oz/½ cup) honey

1½ teaspoons Chinese five-spice
  powder

**1**  **Preheat the oven** to 150°C (300°F/Gas 2).

**2**  **Combine the ingredients** in a small saucepan and warm over low heat.

**3**  **Spread the nuts** onto a large baking tray lined with baking paper and bake for 15–20 minutes, or until golden brown. Cool before serving.

**Note:** You can store the honey-roasted peanuts in an airtight container for up to 1 week.

# SEASONED POPCORN

**MAKES A LARGE BOWL**

60 ml (2 fl oz/¼ cup) oil

150 g (5½ oz/⅔ cup) popping corn

40 g (1½ oz) butter

125 g (4½ oz/⅔ cup) finely chopped
    Kalamata olives

1 bird's eye chilli, finely chopped

1 garlic clove, crushed

1 tablespoon chopped fresh parsley

1 tablespoon chopped fresh oregano

1 teaspoon grated lemon zest

**1  Heat the oil** in a large saucepan, add the popping corn and cover. Cook over medium heat, shaking occasionally, until the popping stops. Transfer to a large bowl and discard any unpopped corn.

**2  Melt the butter** in a large frying pan and add the remaining ingredients. Mix, then toss through the popcorn. Serve warm.

# VEGETABLE CHIPS

## MAKES A LARGE BOWL

500 g (1 lb 2 oz) orange sweet potato

500 g (1 lb 2 oz) beetroot (beets)

500 g (1 lb 2 oz) parsnip

oil, for deep-frying

**1**  Preheat the oven to 180°C (350°F/Gas 4).

**2**  Run a vegetable peeler along the length of the sweet potato and beetroot to make thin ribbons. Cut the parsnip into thin slices.

**3**  Fill a deep, heavy-based saucepan one-third full of oil and heat to 190°C (375°F), or until a cube of bread dropped into the oil browns in 10 seconds. Cook vegetables in batches for about 30 seconds, or until golden and crisp, turning with tongs, if necessary. Drain on crumpled paper towels; season with salt. Keep warm on a baking tray in the oven and cook the remaining chips.

# FRIED CHICKPEAS

## MAKES A LARGE BOWL

275 g (10 oz/1¼ cups) dried chickpeas

oil, for deep-frying

½ teaspoon paprika

¼ teaspoon cayenne pepper

**1** **Soak the chickpeas** overnight in plenty of cold water. Drain well and pat dry with paper towels.

**2** **Fill a deep saucepan** one-third full of oil and heat to 180°C (350°F), or until a cube of bread dropped into the hot oil browns in 15 seconds. Deep-fry half the chickpeas for about 3 minutes. Remove with a slotted spoon, drain on crumpled paper towels and repeat with remaining chickpeas. Partially cover the saucepan as some of the chickpeas may pop. Don't leave the oil unattended at any time.

**3** **Deep-fry the chickpeas** again in batches for 3 minutes each batch, or until browned. Drain well again on crumpled paper towels. Combine the paprika and cayenne pepper with a little salt and sprinkle the mixture over the hot chickpeas. Allow to cool before serving.

# PARMESAN WAFERS

**MAKES 30**

125 g (4½ oz/1¼ cups) good-quality grated parmesan cheese

1 tablespoon plain (all-purpose) flour

2 tablespoons fresh thyme

**1 Preheat the oven** to 220°C (425°F/Gas 7). Line two baking trays with baking paper and, using a 7 cm (2¾ inch) cutter as a guide, draw circles on the paper. Turn the paper upside down on the trays.

**2 Toss cheese and flour** together in a bowl, then sprinkle 2 teaspoons of mixture over 3 or 4 of the circles on the paper, spreading the mixture to the edge of each round. Scatter a few thyme leaves over each round.

**3 Bake in batches** for about 3 minutes, or until melted but not firm. Using a spatula, turn the rounds over and cook for a minute more, or until they are firm and light golden. Remove each round from the tray and drape over a rolling pin or bottle until cool. Repeat with the rest of the ingredients.

# MARINATED OLIVES

MAKES 300 G (12 OZ/2 CUPS)

150 g (6 oz) Kalamata olives

150 g (6 oz) good-quality green olives

185 ml (6 fl oz/¾ cup) extra virgin olive oil

2 sprigs of fresh rosemary

½ tablespoon fresh thyme leaves

2 small red chillies, seeded

several strips lemon zest

2 garlic cloves, bruised

½ teaspoon fennel seeds

2 sprigs of fresh thyme, extra

**1** Place olives, oil, rosemary, thyme, chillies, lemon zest, garlic and fennel in a large saucepan and warm over a low heat. Transfer to a bowl and leave to marinate overnight at room temperature.

**2** Remove the olives from the oil with a slotted spoon and discard the herbs, reserving the oil. Add the extra thyme to the olives before serving.

Note: Serve the oil with bread for dipping.

# MIXED ASIAN CRISPS

**MAKES A LARGE BOWL**

oil, for deep-frying

16 cassava crackers, broken into small
    pieces (see Note)

16 round won ton wrappers

16 small uncooked plain prawn crackers

1 sheet toasted nori, shredded

**1   Fill a deep heavy-based saucepan** or deep-fryer one-third full of oil and heat to 180°C (350°F), or until a cube of bread dropped into the oil browns in 15 seconds.

**2   Deep-fry the cassava pieces** until crisp. Remove with a slotted spoon and drain on crumpled paper towels. Repeat with the won ton wrappers and prawn chips.

**3   When they are all cool,** combine and toss with the nori.

**Note:** Cassava crackers are made from the flour of the dried cassava root. Available from Asian food stores.

# CRISPY ASIAN NOODLE PANCAKES

### MAKES ABOUT 25

150 g (6 oz) dried rice vermicelli noodles

3 tablespoons fresh coriander (cilantro)

3 spring onions (scallions), finely sliced

1 small red chilli, finely chopped

1 stalk lemon grass, white part only, finely chopped

1 garlic clove, crushed

oil, for shallow-frying

**1** Place the noodles in a bowl and cover with boiling water. Stand for 5 minutes, or until soft. Rinse under cold water, drain and dry with paper towels.

**2** Place noodles in a bowl with the coriander, spring onion, chilli, lemon grass and garlic. Season to taste with salt and mix.

**3** Heat the oil in a heavy-based pan and shallow-fry 2 tablespoons of the mixture in hot oil. Flatten with a spatula while cooking and fry until crisp and golden on both sides. Drain the pancakes on paper towels and sprinkle with salt.

# CAYENNE-SPICED ALMONDS

**MAKES 250 G (9 OZ/1⅔ CUPS)**

1½ teaspoons cayenne pepper

1 teaspoon ground cumin

½ teaspoon smoked paprika

½ teaspoon caster (superfine) sugar

2 teaspoons sea salt flakes

1 tablespoon olive oil

250 g (9 oz/1⅔ cups) blanched almonds

**1  Combine the cayenne,** cumin, paprika, sugar and salt in a large bowl and set aside.

**2  Put the oil** and almonds in a saucepan over medium heat and stir for 10 minutes, or until golden. Remove with a slotted spoon, add to the spice mix and toss to combine.

**3  Cool to room temperature,** tossing occasionally and serve.

# WASABI POPCORN

**MAKES 1 LARGE BOWL**

| |
|---|
| 4 tablespoons peanut oil |
| 115 g (4 oz/½ cup) popcorn kernels (popping corn) |
| 1 teaspoon salt |
| 40 g (1½ oz) butter, melted |
| 3 teaspoons wasabi paste |
| 2 teaspoons caster (superfine) sugar |

**1  Heat the oil** in a large saucepan over medium–high heat. Drop a couple of pieces of popcorn kernels into the oil and if they spin, the oil is hot enough to cook the popcorn. Add the kernels and salt and place the lid on the pan.

**2  When you start to hear** the corn pop, shake the pan occasionally until the popping increases, then slows down dramatically. Remove from the heat but keep the lid on until the popping stops completely. Meanwhile, melt the butter in a small saucepan, and stir in the wasabi and sugar. Tip the popcorn into a large bowl and drizzle over half the butter mixture, toss, then add the remaining butter mixture. Season to taste with more salt, if necessary, and serve warm.

# PUFFED CORN MIX

**SERVES 20**

170 g (6 oz/12 cups) puffed corn
  breakfast cereal

400 g (14 oz) packet dried fruit and
  raw nut mix

90 g (3 oz/1¼ cups) unprocessed
  natural bran

55 g (2 oz/1 cup) flaked coconut,
  toasted

60 g (2 oz/⅓ cup) pepitas (pumpkin
  seeds)

250 g (9 oz/¾ cup) honey

**1** **Preheat the oven** to 350°F (180°C/Gas 4). Line 4 baking trays with baking paper. Place the puffed corn, dried fruit and nut mix, bran, coconut and pumpkin seeds in a large bowl and mix together well.

**2** **Heat the honey** in a saucepan over a low heat for about 3 minutes, or until it thins to a pouring consistency. Pour over the puffed corn mixture and stir until all the dry ingredients are well coated with the honey.

**3** **Spread the mixture** on the lined baking trays in a single layer and bake for 15 minutes, or until golden, turning the cereal several times during cooking. Cool completely before storing in an airtight container in a cool, dark place.

**Notes:** If you want to lower the fat content, leave out the flaked coconut. This snack is a great energy booster. It's best eaten at least 30 minutes before or after exercise as the fruit may upset your tummy if you're on the go.

# CURRIED NUTS

MAKES 500 G (1 LB 2 OZ/4½ CUPS)

500 g (1 lb 2 oz) mixed nuts (almonds, brazil nuts, pecan nuts, macadamia nuts, cashew nuts)

1 egg white

2 tablespoons curry powder

1 teaspoon ground cumin

**1  Preheat the oven** to 150°C (300°F/Gas 2). Spread the nuts in a single layer on a baking tray and roast for 10 minutes.

**2  Whisk the egg white** until frothy, then add the nuts, curry powder, cumin and 1 teaspoon salt. Toss together and return to the oven for a further 10–15 minutes, then allow to cool.

# DIPS & DIPPERS

# HUMMUS

**MAKES 660 G (1 LB 8 OZ/3 CUPS)**

220 g (8 oz/1 cup) dried chickpeas

2 tablespoons tahini

4 garlic cloves crushed

2 teaspoons ground cumin

80 ml (3 fl oz/⅓ cup) lemon juice

3 tablespoons olive oil

large pinch cayenne pepper

extra lemon juice, optional

extra olive oil, to garnish

paprika, to garnish

chopped fresh parsley, to garnish

**1** Soak the chickpeas in 1 litre (35 fl oz/4 cups) of water overnight. Drain and place in a large saucepan with 2 litres fresh water (enough to cover the chickpeas by 5 cm/2 inches). Bring to the boil, then reduce the heat and simmer for 1 hour 15 minutes, or until the chickpeas are very tender. Skim any scum from the surface. Drain well, reserve the cooking liquid and leave until cool enough to handle. Pick over for any loose skins and discard.

**2** Process the chickpeas, tahini, garlic, cumin, lemon juice, olive oil, cayenne pepper and 1½ teaspoons salt in a food processor until thick and smooth. With the motor still running, gradually add enough reserved cooking liquid (about 185 ml (6 fl oz/¾ cup)) to form a smooth creamy purée. Season with salt or extra lemon juice.

**3** Spread onto a flat bowl or plate, drizzle with oil, sprinkle with paprika and scatter the parsley over the top. Serve with pitta bread or pide (Turkish/flat bread).

## SERVES 12

2 Lebanese (short) cucumbers

400 g (14 oz/1⅔ cups) low-fat plain yogurt

4 garlic cloves, crushed

3 tablespoons finely chopped mint, plus extra, to garnish

1 tablespoons lemon juice

**1   Cut the cucumbers** in half lengthwise, scoop out the seeds and discard. Leave the skin on and coarsely grate the cucumber into a small colander. Sprinkle with salt and leave over a large bowl for 15 minutes to drain off any bitter juices.

**2   Meanwhile, stir together** the yogurt, garlic, mint and lemon juice.

**3   Rinse the cucumber** under cold water then, taking small handfuls, squeeze out any excess moisture. Combine grated cucumber with the yogurt mixture and season well with salt and freshly ground black pepper. Garnish with mint. Serve with sliced raw carrots, celery, zucchini (courgettes) and unpeeled short (Lebanese cucumbers), and raw cauliflower and broccoli cut into small florets.

**Note:** Tzatziki will keep in an airtight container in the refrigerator for 2–3 days.

# BABA GHANNOUJ (TURKISH EGGPLANT DIP)

**MAKES 375 G (12 OZ/1¾ CUPS)**

2 eggplants (aubergine) (about 1 kg)

3 garlic cloves, crushed

½ teaspoon ground cumin

80 ml (3 fl oz/⅓ cup) lemon juice

2 tablespoons tahini

pinch cayenne pepper

1½ tablespoons olive oil

1 tablespoon finely chopped Italian
   (flat-leaf) parsley

black olives, to garnish

**1** **Preheat oven to** 200°C (400°F/Gas 6). Pierce the eggplants several times with a fork, then cook over an open flame for about 5 minutes, or until skin is black and blistering. Place in a roasting tin and bake for 45 minutes, or until the eggplants are very soft and wrinkled (see Note). Place in a colander over a bowl to drain off any bitter juices. Leave for 30 minutes, or until cool.

**2** **Carefully peel the skin** from the eggplant and discard. Chop flesh and place in a food processor with garlic, cumin, lemon, tahini, cayenne and olive oil. Process until smooth and creamy. Alternatively, use a potato masher or fork. Season with salt and stir in the parsley. Spread onto a flat bowl or plate and garnish with the olives. Serve with flatbread or pide.

**Note:** If you prefer, you can omit the cooking over an open flame and roast the eggplant in a moderately hot 200°C (400°F/Gas 6) oven for about 1 hour, or until very soft and wrinkled.

# TARAMOSALATA

**MAKES 340 G (11 OZ/1½ CUPS)**

5 slices white bread, crusts removed

80 ml (3 fl oz/⅓ cup) milk

100 g (4 oz) tin tarama (mullet roe)

1 egg yolk

½ small onion, grated

1 garlic clove, crushed

2 tablespoons lemon juice

80 ml (3 fl oz/⅓ cup) olive oil

pinch ground white pepper

**1** **Soak the bread** in the milk for 10 minutes. Press in a strainer to extract any excess milk, then place in a food processor with the tarama, egg yolk, onion and garlic. Process for 30 seconds, or until smooth, then add 1 tablespoon lemon juice.

**2** **With the motor running**, slowly pour in the olive oil. The mixture should be smooth and of a dipping consistency. Add the remaining lemon juice and a pinch of white pepper. If the dip tastes too salty, add another piece of bread.

**Variation:** Try smoked cod's roe instead of the mullet roe.

# OLIVE TAPENADE

## MAKES 425 G (16 OZ/1½ CUPS)

400 g (14 fl oz) Kalamata olives, pitted

2 garlic cloves, crushed

2 anchovy fillets in oil, drained

2 tablespoons capers in brine, rinsed, squeezed dry

2 teaspoons chopped fresh thyme

2 teaspoons dijon mustard

1 tablespoon lemon juice

60 ml (2 fl oz/¼ cup) olive oil

1 tablespoon brandy, optional

**1**  **Place olives, crushed** garlic, anchovies, capers, chopped thyme, dijon mustard, lemon juice, olive oil and brandy in a food processor and process until smooth. Season to taste with salt and freshly ground black pepper.

**2**  **Spoon into a clean**, warm jar, cover with a layer of olive oil, seal and refrigerate for up to 1 week.

**3**  **Serve on bruschetta** or with as part of a meze plate.

**Note:** When refrigerated, the olive oil may solidify, making it an opaque white colour. This is a property of olive oil and will not affect the flavour of the dish. Simply bring the dish to room temperature before serving and the olive oil will return to a liquid state.

# AÏOLI WITH CRUDITÉS

SERVES 4

### AÏOLI

4 garlic cloves, crushed

2 egg yolks

315 ml (11 fl oz/1¼ cups) light olive or vegetable oil

1 tablespoon lemon juice

pinch of ground white pepper

12 asparagus spears, trimmed

12 radishes, trimmed

½ telegraph (long) cucumber, seeded, halved lengthways and cut into thick matchsticks

1 head of witlof (chicory), leaves separated

**1** **To make the** aïoli, place the garlic, egg yolks and a pinch of salt in a food processor and process for 10 seconds. With the motor running, add oil in a thin, slow stream. When the mixture starts to thicken, add the oil a little faster. Process until all the oil is incorporated and the mixture is thick and creamy. Stir in the lemon juice and white pepper.

**2** **Bring a saucepan** of water to the boil, add asparagus and cook for 1 minute. Remove asparagus with a slotted spoon and plunge it into a bowl of iced water. Drain.

**3** **Arrange the asparagus,** radish, cucumber and witlof decoratively on a platter and place the aïoli in a bowl on the platter. The aïoli can also be used as a sandwich spread or as a sauce for chicken or fish.

**Note:** It is important that all the ingredients are at room temperature when making this recipe. Should the aïoli start to curdle, beat in 1–2 teaspoons boiling water. If this fails, put another egg yolk in a clean bowl and very slowly whisk the curdled mixture into it, one drop at a time, then continue as above.

# BROAD BEAN DIP

**SERVES 6**

200 g (1 cup) dried broad beans (fava or ful nabed — see Note)

2 garlic cloves, crushed

¼ teaspoon ground cumin

1½ tablespoons lemon juice

up to 75 ml (3 fl oz) olive oil

2 tablespoons chopped flat-leaf (Italian) parsley

flatbread, for serving

**1  Rinse the beans** well, then place in a bowl and cover with 500 ml (17 fl oz/2 cups) of water and leave to soak overnight.

**2  For peeled beans** (see Note), transfer them and their soaking water to a large heavy-based saucepan. For unpeeled beans, drain, then add to the pan with 500 ml (17 fl oz/2 cups) fresh water. Bring to the boil, cover, and simmer for 5–6 hours. Check the water level from time to time and add a little boiling water, as necessary, to keep the beans moist. Do not stir, but shake the pan occasionally to prevent sticking. Set aside to cool slightly. Most of the liquid will have evaporated.

**3  Purée the contents** of the pan in a food processor, then transfer to a bowl and stir in garlic, cumin and lemon juice. Gradually stir in enough olive oil to produce a dipping consistency. As the mixture cools it may become thicker, in which case, stir in a little warm water to return it to a dipping consistency.

**4  Spread over a large dish** and sprinkle with the parsley. Serve with the flatbread, cut into triangles.

**Note:** The fava beans can be the ready-peeled white ones or the small, brown ones.

# POTATO, OLIVE OIL AND GARLIC DIP

**MAKES 550 G (1 LB 2 OZ/2½ CUPS)**

460 g (1 lb/2 cups) mashed potato

3 garlic cloves, crushed

185 ml (6 fl oz/¾ cup) olive oil

2 tablespoons white wine vinegar

5 tablespoons milk

1 very large handful chopped herbs

**1  Combine the potato** and garlic in a bowl. Using electric beaters, gradually beat in half the oil, then the vinegar, then the remaining oil.

**2  Slowly beat in the milk.** Add the herbs and season to taste with salt and freshly ground black pepper.

# CAPSICUM AND WALNUT DIP WITH PITTA WEDGES

SERVES 6–8

4 large red capsicums (peppers)

1 small red chilli

4 garlic cloves, in the skin

100 g (4 oz/1 cup) walnuts, lightly
    toasted

50 g (1¾ oz) sourdough bread,
    crusts removed

2 tablespoons lemon juice

1 tablespoon pomegranate molasses

1 teaspoon ground cumin

pitta bread

olive oil

sea salt

1  **Cut the capsicum** into large flat pieces. Place on a tray skin-side up with the chilli and whole garlic cloves, and cook under a hot grill (broiler) until the skin blackens and blisters. Transfer to a plastic bag and allow to cool. Gently peel away the capsicum and chilli skin, and remove the garlic skins.

2  **Place walnuts in** a food processor and grind fairly finely. Add the capsicum and chilli flesh, garlic, bread, lemon juice, pomegranate molasses and cumin, and blend until smooth. Stir in 2 tablespoons of warm water to even out the texture, and season well with salt. Cover and refrigerate overnight so the flavours develop.

3  **Preheat the oven** to 200°C (400°F/ Gas 6). Cut the pitta bread into wedges, brush with olive oil and lightly sprinkle with sea salt. Cook in the oven for about 5 minutes, or until golden brown. Allow to cool and become crisp.

4  **Drizzle olive oil** over the dip. Serve with the toasted pitta wedges.

# ROASTED EGGPLANT DIP

**SERVES 4**

1 large eggplant (aubergine)

2 teaspoons ground cumin

1 garlic clove, crushed

juice of ½ lemon

2 tablespoons extra virgin olive oil

2 tablespoons chopped coriander
(cilantro) leaves

Lebanese (large pitta) bread, to serve

**1**  **Preheat the oven** to 220°C (425°F/Gas 7). Prick the eggplant several times with a fork and put on a baking tray. Bake for 40–50 minutes, or until the skin is wrinkled and the eggplant appears collapsed. Remove from the oven and set aside to cool.

**2**  **Dry-fry the cumin** in a frying pan over medium heat for 1–2 minutes, or until the colour deepens and the cumin gives off its fragrant aroma. Set aside to cool.

**3**  **Cut open the eggplant**, scoop the flesh into a sieve and drain for 5 minutes. Chop the eggplant flesh until finely diced. Put into a bowl and stir in the cumin, garlic, lemon juice, oil, and coriander and season with salt and pepper to taste.

**4**  **Grill (broil)** the Lebanese bread, cut into fingers and serve with the dip.

# BEETROOT HUMMUS

**SERVES 8**

500 g (1 lb 2 oz) beetroot (beets)

80 ml (3 fl oz/⅓ cup) olive oil

1 large onion, chopped

1 tablespoon ground cumin

400 g (14 oz) tin chickpeas, drained

1 tablespoon tahini

80 g (3 oz/⅓ cup) plain yoghurt

3 garlic cloves, crushed

60 ml (2 fl oz/¼ cup) lemon juice

125 ml (4 fl oz/½ cup) vegetable stock

Lebanese or Turkish bread, to serve

**1**   Scrub the beetroot well. Bring a large saucepan of water to the boil over high heat and cook the beetroot for about 40 minutes, or until soft and cooked through. Drain and cool slightly before peeling.

**2**   Meanwhile, heat 1 tablespoon of the oil in a frying pan over medium heat and cook the onion for 2–3 minutes, or until soft. Add the cumin and cook for a further 1 minute, or until fragrant.

**3**   Chop the beetroot and place in a food processor or blender with the onion mixture, chickpeas, tahini, yoghurt, garlic, lemon juice and stock; process until smooth.

**4**   With the motor running, add the remaining oil in a thin steady stream. Process until the mixture is thoroughly combined. Serve the hummus with Lebanese or Turkish bread.

Note: You can use 500 g (1 lb 2 oz) of any vegetable to make the hummus. Try carrot or pumpkin.

# HERB PEPPER CRISPS WITH BLUE CHEESE DIP

**SERVES 10**

4 sheets lavash or other unleavened bread

90 g (3¼ oz) butter, melted

herb pepper seasoning, to sprinkle

1 tablespoon finely snipped chives

**BLUE CHEESE DIP**

250 g (9 oz) blue vein cheese, chopped

60 g (2¼ oz) butter, softened

1 tablespoon sweet white wine

2 teaspoons chopped mint

1 teaspoon chopped rosemary

2 teaspoons chopped oregano

90 g (3¼ oz/⅓ cup) crème fraîche or sour cream

chives, to garnish

**1**   **Preheat the oven** to 180°C (350°F/Gas 4). Brush each sheet of lavash bread with the butter. Sprinkle with the herb pepper seasoning and chives.

**2**   **Cut each lavash** sheet into 20 squares. Cut each piece in half to make triangles. Place the triangles on baking trays. Bake in batches for 5 minutes, or until crisp. Remove and allow to cool. Serve with the blue cheese dip.

**3**   **For cheese dip,** beat the cheese and butter in a small bowl using electric beaters until smooth and creamy. Add the wine, mint, rosemary and oregano. Mix well. Fold through the crème fraîche or sour cream. Season to taste. Spoon the mixture into serving dishes to serve.

**Note:** The crisps may be stored in an airtight container for up to 2 weeks.

# CHILLI CRAB AND TOMATO

**SERVES 6**

1 small ripe tomato

350 g (12 oz) tinned crabmeat, drained

200 g (7 oz) neufchâtel cheese, softened
(see Note)

2 tablespoons chilli sauce

2 teaspoons tomato paste
(concentrated purée)

1 teaspoon finely grated lemon zest

2 teaspoons lemon juice

1 small onion, finely grated

2 spring onions (scallions), finely sliced

**1**  **Score a cross** in the base of the tomato. Place tomatoes in a heatproof bowl and cover with boiling water. Leave for about 30 seconds, transfer to cold water, then drain and peel the skin away from the cross. Cut the tomato in half, scoop out the seeds with a teaspoon and finely chop the flesh.

**2**  **Squeeze any liquid** from the crabmeat with your hands. Beat the cheese in a bowl with a wooden spoon until smooth, then stir in the crabmeat, chilli sauce, tomato paste, lemon zest, lemon juice and grated onion. Season well with salt and pepper and spoon into a serving bowl.

**3**  **Scatter the spring onion** and tomato over the top. Refrigerate, covered, before serving. Serve the dip with lightly toasted bread if desired.

**Note:** Neufchâtel is a smooth, mild, good-quality cream cheese available from delicatessens. If it is not available, another cream cheese can be used instead.

# PORK AND PEANUT DIP

**SERVES 6–8**

**PASTE**

2 small dried red chillies

2 teaspoons chopped fresh coriander root

3 teaspoons ground white pepper

6 garlic cloves, chopped

4 red Asian shallots, chopped

1 tablespoon peanut oil

300 g (11 oz) minced (ground) pork

2 fresh makrut (kaffir lime) leaves

250 ml (9 fl oz/1 cup) coconut cream

50 g (2 oz/⅓ cup) peanuts, toasted and chopped

1½ tablespoons lime juice

3 tablespoons fish sauce

2 tablespoons grated palm sugar (jaggery) or soft brown sugar

1 tablespoon finely shredded fresh Thai basil or coriander (cilantro) leaves

peanut oil, for deep-frying

150 g (6 oz) cassava crackers

**1** **Soak the chillies** in boiling water for 15 minutes. Remove the seeds and chop. Blend all of the paste ingredients in a food processor until smooth — add water if necessary.

**2** **Heat the oil** in a saucepan. Add the paste and cook, stirring frequently, over medium heat, for 15 minutes, or until the paste darkens. Add the minced pork and stir for 5 minutes, or until coloured. Gradually add the lime leaves and coconut cream, scraping the base of the pan. Cook for 40 minutes, stirring frequently, until the liquid has almost evaporated.

**3** **Add the peanuts,** lime juice, fish sauce and sugar, and cook for 10 minutes, or until the oil begins to separate. Remove from the heat, discard the lime leaves and stir in the basil.

**4** **Fill a deep** heavy-based saucepan one-third full of oil and heat to 180°C (350°F), or until a cube of bread browns in 15 seconds. Break the crackers in half. Deep-fry in small batches until pale, golden and puffed. Remove immediately and drain. Serve with the dip.

**Note:** Cassava crackers are available from Asian food stores.

# PARMESAN PUFF STRAWS

**MAKES 80**

4 sheets ready-rolled puff pastry

50 g (2 oz) butter, melted

165g (6 oz/1⅔ cups) finely grated
   parmesan cheese

1 egg, lightly beaten

**1** **Preheat the oven** to 200°C (400°F/Gas 6).

**2** **Lightly brush the pastry** with the butter, then sprinkle each sheet with 25 g (1 oz/¼ cup) of the cheese and season with salt and pepper.

**3** **Fold each sheet** in half, bringing the top edge down towards you. Brush the tops of each sheet with egg and then sprinkle each one with 2 tablespoons extra grated parmesan and season with salt.

**4** **Using a very sharp knife**, cut the dough vertically into 1 cm (½ inch) wide strips. Transfer each strip to a baking tray lined with baking paper, spacing them evenly. Hold each end of the pastry and stretch and twist in opposite directions.

**5** **Bake in oven** for 10 minutes or until lightly browned.

# TWO-SEED CRACKERS

### MAKES 30

| |
|---|
| 250 g (9 oz/2 cups) plain (all-purpose) flour |
| 1 teaspoon baking powder |
| 2 tablespoons poppy seeds |
| 2 tablespoons sesame seeds |
| 60 g (2 oz) butter, chilled and chopped |
| 125 ml (4 fl oz/½ cup) iced water |

**1** **Preheat the oven** to 180°C (350°F/Gas 4). Line two baking trays with baking paper, or brush lightly with oil. Sift the flour, baking powder and ½ teaspoon salt into a bowl. Add the seeds and season with pepper. Stir to combine. Rub the butter into the flour with your fingertips until the mixture resembles fine breadcrumbs.

**2** **Make a well** in the centre and add almost all the water. Mix together with a flat-bladed knife using a cutting action, adding the remaining water if necessary, until the mixture comes together in soft beads.

**3** **Gather the dough** into a rough ball. Handle the dough gently, and do not knead it. Divide the dough into two portions. Place one portion between two sheets of baking paper and roll to a thickness of 2 mm (1⁄16 inch). Cover the other portion with plastic wrap until needed.

**4** **Using a 6 cm** (2½ inch) round cutter, cut rounds from the dough. Prick all over with a fork and transfer to baking trays. Repeat with the remaining dough. Pile any dough trimmings together (do not knead) and gently re-roll. Cut out more rounds. Bake for 20–25 minutes, or until lightly golden. Transfer to a wire rack to cool. Store in an airtight container for up to 5 days.

# SPICED SOY CRACKERS

**MAKES 24**

155 g (6 oz/1¼ cups) plain (all-purpose) flour

70 g (2 oz/¾ cup) soy flour

½ teaspoon garam masala

½ teaspoon paprika

2½ tablespoons olive oil

2½ tablespoons lemon juice

**1** **Place the flours,** garam masala, paprika and ½ teaspoon salt in a food processor. Add the oil, lemon juice and 100 ml (4 fl oz) water and blend until the mixture comes together in a ball. Cover in plastic wrap and refrigerate for 1 hour.

**2** **Preheat oven to** 160°C (315°F/Gas 2–3). Line 3 baking trays with baking paper. Cut dough into 5 or 6 pieces, then roll each piece into rectangles as thin as possible — 2 mm (1/16 inch). Cut each piece into long, thin triangles 4 x 10 cm/1½ x 4 inch). Place on the prepared trays.

**3** **Bake for 20 minutes,** or until crisp and lightly coloured. Serve with your favourite dip.

# PUFF PASTRY TWISTS

MAKES 96

2 sheets ready-rolled puff pastry, thawed

1 egg, lightly beaten

80 g (3 oz/½ cup) sesame seeds, poppy seeds or caraway seeds

**1** **Preheat the oven** to 200°C (400°F/Gas 6). Lightly grease two baking trays. Brush the pastry with the egg and sprinkle with the sesame seeds.

**2** **Cut the pastry** in half crossways and then into 1 cm (½ inch) wide strips. Twist the strips and place on the greased baking trays. Bake for about 10 minutes, or until golden brown

**Note:** Store in an airtight container for up to 1 week. Refresh in a 180°C (350°F/Gas 4) oven for 2–3 minutes, then allow to cool.

# SPICY POPPADOMS

**MAKES A LARGE BOWL**

3 green cardamom seeds

1½ tablespoons coriander seeds

1 tablespoon cumin seeds

2 cloves

1 teaspoon black peppercorns

1 bay leaf, crushed

1 teaspoon ground mace

¼ teaspoon ground cinnamon

pinch of ground chilli

oil, for deep-frying

24 large poppadoms, broken
   into quarters

**1**  **Toast the cardamom,** coriander and cumin seeds, cloves, peppercorns and bay leaf in a dry frying pan over low heat for 2–3 minutes, or until richly fragrant. Cool for 5 minutes, then grind to a fine powder. Stir in the mace, cinnamon and chilli.

**2**  **Fill a wide,** large saucepan one-third full with oil and heat to 180°C (350°F), or until a cube of bread dropped into the oil browns in 15 seconds. Deep-fry the pieces of poppadom, a few at a time, until crisp and golden.

**3**  **Drain on crumpled paper** towels and sprinkle with the spice mix while still hot.

# HERBED LAVASH

### MAKES ABOUT 48 PIECES

125 ml (4 fl oz/½ cup) olive oil

3 garlic cloves, crushed

6 slices lavash or other unleavened bread

2 teaspoons sea salt flakes

2 teaspoons dried mixed Italian herbs

**1** Preheat the oven to 180°C (350°F/Gas 4).

**2** Heat the oil and garlic in a small saucepan over low heat until the oil is warm and the garlic is fragrant but not browned.

**3** Brush the lavash bread on both sides with the garlic oil. Cut each piece of bread into eight triangular wedges and position side-by-side on baking trays. Sprinkle the upper side with the sea salt and herbs. Bake the lavash for 8–10 minutes, or until crisp.

# HERB GRISSINI

## MAKES 24

7 g (¼ oz) sachet dried yeast

1 teaspoon sugar

500 g (1 lb 2 oz/4 cups) plain (all-purpose) flour

60 ml (2 fl oz/¼ cup) olive oil

5 tablespoons chopped flat-leaf (Italian) parsley

5 tablespoons chopped basil

2 teaspoons sea salt flakes

**1  Combine the yeast,** sugar and 315 ml (11 fl oz/1¼ cups) warm water in a small bowl and leave in a warm place for 5–10 minutes, or until foamy.

**2  Sift the flour** and 1 teaspoon salt into a bowl. Stir in the yeast and oil to form a dough, adding more water, if necessary. Gather into a ball and turn out onto a lightly floured surface. Knead for 10 minutes, or until soft and elastic. Add herbs and knead for 1–2 minutes to incorporate evenly. Place the dough in a lightly oiled bowl and cover with plastic wrap. Leave in a warm place for 1 hour, or until doubled in volume. Preheat the oven to 230°C (450°F/Gas 8) and lightly grease two large baking trays.

**3  Punch down the dough** and knead for 1 minute. Divide into 24 portions, and roll each portion into a 30 cm (12 inch) long stick. Place on the trays and lightly brush with water. Sprinkle with the salt flakes. Bake for 15 minutes, or until crisp and golden.

**Note:** Ideal with white bean dip or hummus (see page 24).

# DEEP-FRIED CHEESE RAVIOLI

oil, for deep-frying

300 g (11 oz) fresh cheese ravioli (see Note)

**1** **Fill a deep** heavy-based saucepan or deep-fryer one-third full of oil and heat to 180°C (350°F), or until a cube of bread dropped into the oil browns in 15 seconds. Cook the ravioli in batches until golden brown.

**2** **Remove from the oil** and drain on crumpled paper towels. Sprinkle with salt and cracked black pepper, and serve hot.

**Note:** If you can't find fresh ravioli in sheets, individual pieces will work equally well.

# TORTILLA SHARDS

**SERVES 8–10**

2 tablespoons sweet paprika

¼ teaspoon cayenne pepper

oil, for deep-frying

8 large flour tortillas, cut into long
   triangles

**1   Combine sweet paprika** and the cayenne pepper in a small bowl.

**2   Fill a deep** heavy-based saucepan one-third full of oil and heat to 180°C (350°F), or until a cube of bread dropped into the oil browns in 15 seconds. Drop the tortilla shards in the oil in batches and deep-fry until crisp. Drain on crumpled paper towels and sprinkle lightly with the paprika mix while still hot.

# ORANGE SWEET POTATO WEDGES

## SERVES 6–8

1.3 kg (3 lbs) orange sweet potato, peeled and sliced into 6 cm x 2 cm (3 x 1 inch) wedges

2 tablespoons olive oil

1 tablespoon fennel seeds

1 tablespoon coriander seeds

½ teaspoon cayenne pepper

1 teaspoon sea salt flakes

**1** **Preheat the oven** to 200°C (400°F/Gas 6).

**2** **Place the sweet potato** in a large baking dish and toss with the oil.

**3** **In a mortar and pestle**, pound together the fennel and coriander seeds until they are roughly crushed. Add to the orange sweet potato along with the cayenne and sea salt flakes. Toss well and then bake for about 30 minutes, or until browned and crisp. Serve warm.

# SPRING ONION FLATBREADS

**MAKES 40**

2 teaspoons oil

185 g (7 oz) spring onions (scallions), thinly sliced

1 garlic clove, crushed

½ teaspoon grated fresh ginger

215 g (8 oz/1¾ cups) plain (all-purpose) flour

1½ tablespoons chopped coriander (cilantro)

oil, for shallow-frying

**1**  Heat the oil in a frying pan, and cook the spring onion, garlic and ginger for 2–3 minutes, or until soft.

**2**  Combine the flour and 1 teaspoon salt in a bowl. Stir in the spring onion mixture and the chopped coriander. Gradually stir in 250 ml (9 fl oz/1 cup) boiling water, stopping when a loose dough forms. Knead the dough with floured hands for 1½–2 minutes, or until smooth. Cover with plastic wrap and rest for 30 minutes. Break off walnut-sized pieces of dough and roll them out into thin ovals.

**3**  Fill a large frying pan with 2 cm (1 inch) oil and heat over medium heat. When shimmering, cook the breads 2–3 at a time for 25–30 seconds each side, or until crisp and golden. Drain on paper towels and serve warm.

# SUN-DRIED TOMATO PLAITS

**MAKES 8**

1 sheet frozen puff pastry, thawed

1 egg, beaten

40 g (1½ oz) semi-dried (sun-blushed) tomatoes, sliced

**1  Preheat the oven** to 210°C (415°F/Gas 6–7). Lightly grease a baking tray.

**2  Lay the sheet** of puff pastry on a work surface and brush lightly with the egg. Cut into 1 cm (½ inch) strips. Join three strips together at the top, by pressing. Plait them together, inserting slices of semi-dried tomato at intervals in the plait.

**3  Place the plaits** on the baking tray and bake for about 12 minutes, or until puffed and golden. When completely cool, store in an airtight container.

# CARAWAY AND PARMESAN GRISSINI

**MAKES 40**

2 teaspoons dried yeast

1 teaspoon caster (superfine) sugar

350 g (12 oz/2¾ cups) strong flour

½ teaspoon salt

2 tablespoons caraway seeds

2 tablespoons olive oil

1 lightly beaten egg, for glazing

50 g (2 oz/½ cup) grated parmesan cheese, for sprinkling

2 teaspoons sea salt flakes, for sprinkling

**1**  **Dissolve the yeast** and sugar in 3 tablespoons of lukewarm water.

**2**  **Put the flour,** salt and 1 tablespoon of caraway seeds into a large bowl. Make a well in the centre, and pour in the yeast mixture, 185 ml (6 fl oz/¾ cup) of lukewarm water and olive oil. Mix to a soft dough.

**3**  **Turn out the dough** onto a floured surface and knead for 5 minutes, or until smooth and elastic. Return to a lightly oiled bowl, cover and leave to rise in a warm place for 1 hour, or until doubled in size.

**4**  **Knock back and divide** the dough into 40 equal portions. Roll the dough into cigar shapes about 20 cm (8 inches) long. Place shapes on oiled baking trays. Allow to rise for 15 minutes. Preheat the oven to 200°C (400°F/Gas 6).

**5**  **Brush with the beaten egg,** and sprinkle with remaining caraway seeds, parmesan and sea salt flakes. Bake for about 30 minutes, or until crisp and golden.

# BASIL AND CHEESE GRISSINI

**MAKES 24**

7 g (¼ oz) sachet dry yeast

1 teaspoon sugar

500 g (1 lb 2 oz/4 cups) plain (all-purpose) flour

60 ml (2 fl oz/¼ cup) olive oil

4 tablespoons chopped basil

50 g (2 oz/½ cup) finely grated parmesan cheese

2 teaspoons sea salt flakes

**1  Combine the yeast,** sugar and 315 ml (11 fl oz/1¼ cups) warm water in a bowl and leave in a warm place for about 10 minutes, or until foamy. Sift the flour and 1 teaspoon salt into a bowl. Stir yeast and oil into the flour to form a dough, adding a little more water if necessary.

**2  Gently gather the dough** into a ball and turn out onto a lightly floured surface. Knead for 10 minutes, or until soft and elastic. Add the basil and parmesan, and knead for 1–2 minutes to incorporate evenly.

**3  Place the dough** in a lightly oiled bowl and cover with plastic wrap. Leave in a warm place for 1 hour, or until doubled in volume. Preheat the oven to 230°C (450°F/Gas 8) and lightly grease two large baking trays.

**4  Punch down the dough** and knead for 1 minute. Divide into 24 portions, and roll each portion into a 30 cm (12 inch) long stick. Place on the trays and brush with water. Sprinkle with salt flakes. Bake for 15 minutes, or until crisp and golden.

# COLD FINGERFOOD

# OYSTERS WITH LEMON HERB DRESSING

**MAKES 24**

24 fresh oysters (see Notes)

1 tablespoon chopped fresh dill

1 garlic clove, crushed

1 tablespoon finely chopped fresh flat-
    leaf (Italian) parsley

2 teaspoons finely snipped fresh chives

2 tablespoons lemon juice

60 ml (2 fl oz/¼ cup) extra virgin
    olive oil

chive bows, to garnish

brown bread, cubed, to garnish

**1**  **Remove the oysters** from the shells; pat dry. Wash the shells, replace oysters and cover with a damp cloth. Place in the refrigerator.

**2**  **Place the dill,** garlic, parsley, chives, lemon juice and oil in a bowl and season to taste with salt and cracked black pepper. Combine thoroughlhy, then drizzle a little of the dressing over each oyster.

**3**  **Add chive bows** and serve with cubes of brown bread.

**Notes:** Oysters are sold freshly shucked on the half shell, or alive and unshucked. When buying fresh shucked oysters, look for a plump, moist oyster. The flesh should be creamy with a clear liquid (oyster liquor) surrounding it. Oysters should smell like the fresh sea and have no traces of shell particles.

If you prefer to shuck the oysters yourself, look for tightly closed, unbroken shells.

Oysters are often served on a bed of rock salt or crushed ice to help them remain stable and upright, and to keep them cool in hot weather.

# OYSTERS WITH TOMATO AND CORIANDER SALSA

MAKES 24

2 vine-ripened tomatoes, seeded
  and finely diced

2 French shallots, finely chopped

2 small fresh red chillies, seeded
  and sliced

3 tablespoons chopped coriander
  (cilantro)

1 tablespoon lime juice

24 prepared oysters

**1** **Place the tomato,** shallots, chilli and coriander in a bowl
and mix together well. Stir in the lime juice, then season with
salt and pepper. Place a teaspoon of the salsa on each oyster.

# CUCUMBER CUPS WITH THAI BEEF SALAD

MAKES 24

4 Lebanese (short) cucumbers

oil, for pan-frying

250 g (9 oz) fillet steak

1 small red onion, finely chopped

20 fresh mint leaves, finely chopped

1 tablespoon finely chopped coriander (cilantro) leaves

1½ tablespoons fish sauce

1½ tablespoons lime juice

1 bird's eye chilli, seeded and finely chopped

1 teaspoon grated palm sugar (jaggery) or soft brown sugar

small coriander (cilantro) leaves, to garnish

**1** **Trim each end** of the cucumbers but do not peel them. Cut each cucumber into 2 cm (1 inch) thick slices; you should get 24 pieces. Scoop out the centre of each slice with a melon baller, leaving a shell of flesh.

**2** **Heat a large frying** pan over high heat and brush lightly with oil. Season the beef with salt and pepper, then place in the pan and cook for 1½–2 minutes each side, depending on the thickness (the beef needs to be rare). Set aside to rest for 5 minutes. Thinly slice beef across the grain, then slice each piece into 5 mm (¼ inch) wide strips and transfer to a bowl.

**3** **Add the onion,** mint and coriander to the bowl and mix well. Combine fish sauce, lime juice, chilli and sugar, stirring until the sugar has dissolved. Pour over the beef mixture and mix well. Fill each cucumber cup with the Thai beef salad and garnish with a whole coriander leaf.

Note: The cups can be prepared a day ahead. To store them, directly cover the surface with plastic wrap to prevent them from drying out. Store in an airtight container. The meat can also be cooked a day early, but do not slice it until you are ready to assemble the salad.

# VEGETABLE SHAPES WITH SOUR CREAM AND LEEK

**MAKES 35**

2 x 425 g (16 oz) long thin orange sweet potatoes, peeled

5 beetroots (beets)

125 g (5 oz/½ cup) sour cream or crème fraîche

1 garlic clove, crushed

¼ teaspoon finely grated lime zest

oil, for deep-frying

2 leeks, cut into thin 5 cm (2 inch) long strips

**1**  Put the orange sweet potato in one large saucepan of water and put the beetroots in another. Bring them to the boil over high heat and simmer, covered, for 30–40 minutes, or until tender, adding more boiling water if it starts to evaporate. Drain separately and set aside until cool enough to handle. Remove the skins from the beetroots. Trim the ends from the beetroots and sweet potatoes and cut both into 1 cm (½ inch) slices. Using a biscuit cutter, cut the thin slices into shapes. Leave to drain on paper towels.

**2**  Place the sour cream, garlic and lime zest in a bowl and combine well. Refrigerate until ready to use.

**3**  Fill a deep heavy-based saucepan or deep-fryer one-third full of oil and heat to 190°C (375°F), or until a bread cube dropped into the oil browns in 10 seconds. Cook the leek in four batches for 30 seconds, or until lightly golden and crisp. Drain on crumpled paper towels and season to taste with some salt.

**4**  To assemble, place a teaspoon of the sour cream mixture on top of each vegetable shape and top with some fried leek.

# CHERRY TOMATO AND BOCCONCINI TARTLETS

MAKES 30

250 g (9 oz/2 cups) plain (all-purpose) flour

125 g (5 oz) chilled butter, chopped

1 egg

FILLING

300 g (11 oz/2 cups) cherry tomatoes, quartered

2 tablespoons olive oil

1 garlic clove, crushed

200 g (7 oz) bocconcini, quartered

80 g (3 oz/½ cup) chopped Kalamata olives

1 tablespoon extra virgin olive oil

1 tablespoon torn fresh basil

oil, for deep-frying

30 small fresh basil leaves

**1** **Preheat the oven** to 200°C (400°F/Gas 6). Grease 30 mini muffin holes. Sift the flour and rub in the butter with fingertips until the mixture resembles fine breadcrumbs. Make a well, add the egg and mix with a flat-bladed knife, using a cutting action, until the dough gathers in beads. Add a little cold water if necessary. Press the dough into a ball, wrap in plastic wrap and chill for about 30 minutes.

**2** **Roll out dough** between two sheets of baking paper to 2 mm (1/16 inch) thick and cut 30 rounds with a 6 cm (2 inch) cutter. Press a round into each muffin hole. Prick each base with a fork and bake for 6 minutes, or until dry and golden. If they should puff up, use a clean tea towel (dish towel) to press them back. Cool.

**3** **To make filling,** preheat the oven to 200°C (400°F/Gas 6). Combine tomatoes, olive oil and garlic in a roasting tin and bake for 15 minutes, or until golden. Cool, add the bocconcini, olives, extra virgin olive oil and the torn basil leaves Season, and toss to combine.

**4** **Fill a pan** one-third full of oil and heat to 180°C (350°F), or until a cube of bread browns in 15 seconds. Deep-fry small basil leaves in batches for about 30 seconds, or until crisp. Drain. Spoon vegetable filling into the pastry cases and top with a fried basil leaf.

# SMOKED SALMON BREAD BASKETS

### MAKES 24

250 g (9 oz) smoked salmon

1 loaf white sliced bread

60 ml (2 fl oz/¼ cup) olive oil

90 g (3 oz/⅓ cup) whole-egg mayonnaise

2 teaspoons extra virgin olive oil

1 teaspoon white wine vinegar

1 teaspoon finely chopped dill

3 teaspoons horseradish cream

3 tablespoons salmon roe

fresh dill sprigs, to garnish

**1** **Preheat the oven** to 180°C (350°F/Gas 4). Cut the salmon into 2 cm (1 inch) wide strips. Flatten the bread very thinly with a rolling pin, then cut out 24 rounds with a 7 cm (3 inch) cutter. Brush both sides of the rounds with oil and push into the holes of two 12-hole flat-based mini muffin tins. Bake for 10 minutes, or until crisp. Cool.

**2** **Stir the mayonnaise** in a bowl with the extra virgin olive oil, vinegar, dill and horseradish until combined.

**3** **Arrange folds of salmon** in each cooled bread case and top each one with 1 teaspoon of mayonnaise mixture. Spoon ½ teaspoon of salmon roe on top of each and garnish with dill.

**Note:** The bread cases can be made a day in advance. When completely cold, store in an airtight container. If they soften, you can crisp them on a baking tray in a 180°C (350°F/Gas 4) oven for 5 minutes. Cool before filling.

# SAVOURY SHORTBREAD WITH TOMATO JAM

**MAKES 48**

## TOMATO JAM

5 vine-ripened tomatoes, quartered

1 teaspoon fennel seeds

½ teaspoon cumin seeds

1 small red onion

2 garlic cloves

100 ml (4 fl oz) olive oil

1½ tablespoons soft brown sugar

1½ tablespoons red wine vinegar

## SHORTBREAD

250 g (9 oz) butter, at room temperature

1 tablespoon hot water

405g (14 oz) plain (all-purpose) flour

½ teaspoon sweet paprika

300 g (11 oz) bacon, finely chopped

125 g (5 oz/1¼ cups) grated parmesan cheese

60 g poppy seeds

small fresh basil leaves, to garnish

**1  Preheat the oven** to 180°C (350°F/Gas 4). Place the tomatoes on a roasting tray and roast for 30 minutes. Cool slightly, then purée in a blender or food processor until just smooth. Toast fennel and cumin seeds in a dry frying pan for 1–2 minutes, or until fragrant. Cool slightly, then grind the seeds to a powder.

**2  Purée the onion,** garlic, ground spices and half the olive oil in a food processor until well combined.

**3  Heat the remaining** olive oil in a large saucepan and cook the onion mixture over low heat for 25–30 minutes, or until the onion is just beginning to caramelize. Add the sugar and vinegar and cook for a further 2 minutes, then stir in the tomato mixture. Cook over very low heat, stirring occasionally, for 1–1½ hours, or until the paste is thick and there is very little liquid remaining. Remove from the heat and allow to cool.

**4  To make the shortbread,** beat the butter in a bowl until pale. Gradually add the hot water. Sift the flour and paprika into the bowl and mix with a wooden spoon until smooth. Stir in the bacon, parmesan and 60 ml (2 fl oz/¼ cup) water, then season well with cracked black pepper, adding more water if necessary. Roll into four logs 3 cm (1¼ inch) thick. Wrap in plastic wrap and refrigerate for 2 hours. Spread poppy seeds on a work surface; roll logs in them until evenly coated.

**5  Preheat oven** to 170°C (325°F/Gas 3) and lightly grease two baking trays. Slice logs into 5 mm (¼ inch) thick slices. Place on the prepared trays and bake for 15–18 minutes, or until pale and crisp. Cool completely.

**6  To serve the shortbread,** top with 1 teaspoon tomato jam and a small basil leaf. (Shortbread can be made 1 week ahead. Jam will keep for 4 weeks in a container in the refrigerator.)

# HERBED PIKELETS WITH PEAR AND BLUE CHEESE TOPPING

**MAKES 36**

125 g (5 oz/1 cup) self-raising flour

2 eggs, lightly beaten

125 ml (4 fl oz/½ cup) milk

2 tablespoons finely chopped parsley

2 teaspoons finely chopped sage

### PEAR AND BLUE CHEESE TOPPING

100 g (4 oz) Blue Castello or other creamy blue cheese

75 g (3 oz) cream cheese

2 teaspoons brandy

1 large ripe green-skinned pear

30 g (1 oz/¼ cup) toasted walnuts, finely chopped

½ lemon

chopped chives, for garnish

**1**  Sift the flour into a bowl and make a well in the centre. Gradually add the combined eggs and milk, mixing the flour in slowly. When the flour is incorporated, add the parsley and sage and season well. Whisk until a smooth batter forms.

**2**  Heat a large non-stick frying pan over medium heat and spray with cooking oil spray. Drop heaped teaspoons of batter into the pan and flatten them to give 5 cm (2 inch) circles. Cook until bubbles appear in the surface of the pikelet, then turn and brown the other side. Lift out to cool on a wire rack.

**3**  To make the topping, beat cheeses and brandy together until smooth. Season with pepper. Cut the pear in half and peel and core one half, then dice it into 5 mm (¼ inch) pieces, leaving the other half untouched. Stir diced pear and walnuts into the cheese mixture. Core the other half of the pear but do not peel. Thinly slice the pear lengthways. Cut each slice into 2 cm (¾ inch) triangles with green skin on one side. Squeeze lemon juice over the cut surfaces to prevent discolouration.

**4**  Spread 1 teaspoon of topping on each pikelet. Arrange three pear triangles on top and garnish with chives.

# CHICKEN LIVER PARFAIT

**MAKES 48**

35 g (1 oz) butter

2 French shallots, peeled and sliced

500 g (1 lb 2 oz) chicken livers, trimmed

60 ml (2 fl oz/¼ cup) thick (double/ heavy) cream

1 tablespoon cognac or brandy

48 Melba toasts

8 cornichons (baby gherkins), thinly sliced on the diagonal

**1**  Heat a large frying pan over medium heat. Melt butter, then add the shallots to the pan and cook, stirring, for about 5 minutes, or until they are soft and transparent. Use a slotted spoon to transfer them to a food processor.

**2**  In the same pan, add chicken livers and cook in batches over a high heat, stirring, for 4–5 minutes, or until seared on the outside but still pink and quite soft on the inside. Add to the food processor with 2 tablespoons of the pan juices, the cream, cognac and some salt and pepper. Blend for about 5 minutes, or until quite smooth. Push through a fine sieve to remove any remaining lumps. Transfer to a serving dish, put plastic wrap directly on the surface of the mixture and refrigerate for at least 4 hours, or until well chilled.

**3**  To serve, spoon a heaped teaspoon of parfait onto each Melba toast and top with a slice of cornichon. Alternatively, leave the parfait in the serving dish, supply a small knife and allow guests to help themselves.

**Note**: The parfait can be made up to 3 days in advance and stored in the fridge in an airtight container. Assemble no more than 30 minutes before serving.

# SMOKED TROUT PUFFS

**MAKES 36**

1 sheet frozen puff pastry, thawed

1 egg, beaten

sesame seeds, for sprinkling

250 g (9 oz/1 cup) light cream cheese

2 tablespoons capers, rinsed, drained and finely chopped

2 spring onions (scallions), finely chopped

2 tablespoons chopped dill

320 g (11 oz) whole smoked trout, skinned, bones removed and flaked

**1    Preheat the oven** to 220°C (425°F/Gas 7). Lightly grease two baking trays. Cut 36 small squares from the sheet of puff pastry. Brush the tops lightly with the beaten egg and sprinkle with the sesame seeds.

**2    Place on the baking trays** and bake for about 8 minutes, or until puffed and well browned. Allow to cool, then gently split in half horizontally.

**3    Soften the cream cheese** and blend with the capers, spring onion and dill. Spread on the bases of the squares, top with some smoked trout, then replace the pastry tops at a slight angle.

# MEXICAN BITES

**MAKES 36**

2 x 400 g tins kidney beans, drained

1 teaspoon ground cumin

2 tablespoons olive oil

¼ teaspoon cayenne pepper

1 avocado

1 small garlic clove, crushed

2 tablespoons sour cream

2 tablespoons lime juice

1 vine-ripened tomato, seeded and finely chopped

2 tablespoons finely chopped coriander

250 g (9 oz) packet round tortilla chips

**1   To make the refried beans**, put the kidney beans in a bowl and mash well with a potato masher, then add the cumin. Heat 1½ tablespoons of oil in a large non-stick frying pan and add the cayenne pepper and mashed kidney beans. Cook over medium–high heat for about 3 minutes, stirring constantly. Allow to cool. Refrigerate for about 30 minutes, or until cold.

**2   Scoop the avocado** flesh into a food processor and add the garlic, sour cream and 1 tablespoon of the lime juice. Process for a few minutes until it is a thick creamy paste, then add salt to taste. Refrigerate.

**3   To make the salsa**, mix together the tomato, coriander and the remaining olive oil and lime juice in a bowl. Refrigerate until needed.

**4   To assemble**, lay out 36 round tortilla chips. Put a heaped teaspoon of refried beans in the centre of each chip, add a teaspoon of the avocado cream and lastly half a teaspoon of tomato salsa.

**Note:** The bean purée can be made 3 days in advance. Make the salsa up to 2 hours beforehand. Assemble just before serving.

# HERBED CHEESE TARTLETS

**MAKES 48**

### PASTRY

| |
|---|
| 500 g (1 lb 2 oz/4 cups) plain (all-purpose) flour |
| 1 teaspoon paprika |
| 250 g (9 oz) butter, chopped |
| 80 ml (2½ fl oz/⅓ cup) lemon juice |
| 160–200 ml (6–7 fl oz) iced water |

### FILLING

| |
|---|
| 500 g (1 lb 2 oz) cottage cheese |
| 2 tablespoons chopped chervil, plus extra, to garnish |
| 2 tablespoons chopped tarragon |
| 2 teaspoons snipped chives |
| 125 ml (4 fl oz/½ cup) thick (double/heavy) cream |
| 24 black olives, pitted and sliced |

**1  To make the pastry**, sift the flour, paprika and a pinch of salt into a large bowl. Add butter and rub into the flour using your fingertips, until the mixture resembles fine breadcrumbs. Make a well in the centre and stir in the lemon juice and the iced water. Mix with a flat-bladed knife until the mixture comes together in beads. Gently gather together and lift out onto a lightly floured surface. Flatten into a disc, wrap in plastic wrap and refrigerate for 15 minutes.

**2  Preheat the oven** to 200°C (400°F/Gas 6). Grease two 12-hole round-based mini muffin tins. Roll the dough out on a lightly floured surface to 3 mm (⅛ inch) thick and, using an 8 cm (3 inch) cutter, cut 24 rounds from the pastry and line the muffin tins. Bake for 8–10 minutes, or until golden brown. Repeat with the remaining pastry.

**3  To make the filling**, beat together the cottage cheese, herbs and cream until smooth. Stir in the olives with some salt and black pepper. Spoon into the cases and garnish with chervil and black pepper.

# ASPARAGUS AND PROSCIUTTO BUNDLES WITH HOLLANDAISE

MAKES 24 BUNDLES

24 spears fresh asparagus, trimmed

8 slices prosciutto, cut into thirds lengthways

HOLLANDAISE

175 g (6 oz) butter

4 egg yolks

1 tablespoon lemon juice

ground white pepper

**1** **Blanch asparagus in** boiling salted water for 2 minutes, then drain and refresh in cold water. Pat dry, then cut the spears in half. Lay the bottom half of each spear next to its tip, then secure by wrapping a piece of prosciutto around them.

**2** **To make the hollandaise,** melt the butter in a small saucepan. Skim any froth off the top. Cool the butter a little. Combine the egg yolks and 2 tablespoons of water in a small heatproof bowl placed over a saucepan of simmering water, making sure the base of the bowl does not touch the water. Using a wire whisk, beat for about 3–4 minutes, or until the

mixture is thick and foamy. Make sure the bowl does not get too hot or you will end up with scrambled eggs. Add the butter slowly, a little at a time at first, whisking well between each addition. Keep adding the butter in a thin stream, whisking continuously, until all the butter has been used. Try to avoid using the milky whey in the bottom of the pan, but don't worry if a little gets in. Stir in the lemon juice and season with salt and white pepper. Place in a bowl and serve warm with the asparagus.

# DOLMADES

**MAKES 48**

200 g (7 oz) packet vine leaves in brine

250 g (9 oz/1 cup) medium-grain rice

1 small onion, finely chopped

1 tablespoon olive oil

50 g (2 oz/⅓ cup) pine nuts, toasted

2 tablespoons currants

2 tablespoons chopped fresh dill

2 tablespoons finely chopped fresh mint

2 tablespoons finely chopped flat-leaf
(Italian) parsley

80 ml (3 fl oz/⅓ cup) olive oil, extra

2 tablespoons lemon juice

500 ml (17 fl oz/2 cups) chicken or
vegetable stock

**1** **Cover the vine leaves** with cold water and soak them for 15 minutes. Pat dry and cut off any stems. Reserve 5–6 leaves; discard any with holes. Meanwhile, pour boiling water over the rice and soak for 10 minutes, then drain.

**2** **Place the rice,** onion, oil, pine nuts, currants, herbs and salt and pepper in a large bowl, and mix well.

**3** **Lay some leaves** vein-side-down on a flat surface and place ½ tablespoon of filling in the middle of each leaf. Fold the stalk end over the filling, then the left and right sides into the middle, and finally roll firmly towards the tip. The dolmade should resemble a small cigar. Repeat to make 48 dolmades.

**4** **Line the base** of a large, heavy-based saucepan or flameproof casserole dish with the reserved leaves. Drizzle with 1 tablespoon of the extra oil. Put the dolmades in the pan, packing them tightly in one layer. Pour the remaining oil and lemon juice over them.

**5** **Pour the stock** over the dolmades and cover with an inverted plate to stop them moving while cooking. Bring to the boil, then reduce the heat and simmer gently, covered, for 45 minutes. Remove with a slotted spoon. Serve warm or cold.

# MINI QUICHES LORRAINES

**MAKES 24**

3 sheets frozen shortcrust (pie) pastry, thawed

60 g (2¼ oz) gruyère cheese, grated

30 g (1 oz) butter

2 bacon slices, finely chopped

1 onion, finely chopped

2 eggs

185 ml (6 fl oz/¾ cup) pouring cream

½ teaspoon freshly grated nutmeg

chives, cut into short strips

**1  Preheat the oven** to 190°C (375°F/Gas 5). Lightly grease two 12-hole round-based mini muffin tins. With a plain 8 cm (3 inch) cutter, cut rounds of pastry and fit in the tins. Divide cheese evenly among the pastry bases. Cover and refrigerate while making the filling.

**2  Heat the butter** in a small frying pan and cook the bacon and onion for 2–3 minutes, or until tender. Drain on paper towels. When cool, divide the mixture evenly among the bases. Whisk the eggs in a bowl with the cream, nutmeg and a little freshly ground black pepper. Pour or spoon carefully over the bacon mixture.

**3  Put a few strips** of chive on top of each quiche. Bake for 20 minutes, or until filling is lightly browned and set. Serve at room temperature.

**Note:** These quiches can be cooked up to 2 days ahead and stored in an airtight container in the refrigerator. They can be frozen in single layers for up to 2 months. Reheat in a 180°C (350°F/Gas 4) oven.

# CAPSICUM ROLLED WITH GOAT'S CHEESE

SERVES 4

4 large red capsicums (peppers)

2 tablespoons flat-leaf (Italian) parsley, chopped

2 tablespoons chives, snipped

2 tablespoons baby capers, finely chopped

1 tablespoon balsamic vinegar

150 g (5½ oz) goat's cheese

16 basil leaves

olive oil, to cover

crusty Italian bread, to serve

**1   Cut the capsicum** into large flat pieces and remove any seeds. Place on a tray skin-side up under a hot grill (broiler) until the skin blisters and blackens. Place in a plastic bag and leave to cool, then peel away the skin. Cut into 3 cm (1¼ inch) wide pieces.

**2   Combine the parsley,** chives, capers and balsamic vinegar in a small bowl. Crumble in the goat's cheese, and mix well. Then season with a generous amount of freshly ground black pepper. Place a basil leaf on the inside of each capsicum piece, and top with a teaspoon of the goat's cheese mixture. Roll the capsicum over the goat's cheese and secure with a toothpick.

**3   Place in an** airtight, non-reactive container and cover with olive oil. Refrigerate until required. Allow to return to room temperature before serving with crusty Italian bread.

# CAPSICUM MUFFINS WITH TAPENADE AND MASCARPONE

**MAKES 24**

1 red capsicum (pepper)

250 g (9 oz/2 cups) plain (all-purpose) flour

3 teaspoons baking powder

75g (3 oz/¾ cup) grated parmesan cheese

125 ml (4 fl oz/½ cup) milk

2 eggs, lightly beaten

60 ml (2 fl oz/¼ cup) olive oil

1½ tablespoons olive oil, extra

75 g (3 oz/⅓ cup) mascarpone cheese

24 fresh basil leaves

TAPENADE

80 g (3 oz/½ cup) pitted Kalamata olives

1 garlic clove, chopped

2 anchovies (optional)

2 teaspoons drained capers

2 tablespoons olive oil

2 teaspoons lemon juice

**1** **Cut the capsicum** into large flattish pieces. Cook, skin-side-up, under a hot grill (broiler) until the skin blackens and blisters. Place in a plastic bag and allow to cool. Peel off the skin and finely chop the flesh.

**2** **Preheat the oven** to 180°C (350°F/Gas 4). Lightly grease 24 non-stick mini muffin holes. Sift the flour and baking powder into a bowl, then add the capsicum and parmesan. Season with salt and pepper. Make a well in the centre.

**3** **Pour the combined milk**, eggs and oil into the well. Fold gently with a metal spoon until just combined. Do not overmix—the batter should be lumpy. Overmixing produces tough muffins.

**4** **Fill each muffin** hole with mixture. Bake 15–20 minutes, or until a skewer comes out clean. Cool slightly. Loosen each muffin with a flat-bladed knife then lift out onto a wire rack.

**5** **To make tapenade,** place the olives, garlic, anchovies and capers in a food processor. Blend until finely chopped, then, while the motor is running, add the oil and lemon juice to form a paste. Season with pepper.

**6** **Heat the extra** oil in a saucepan and fry the basil leaves until they are just crisp. Remove and drain on paper towels.

**7** **While still warm,** cut the tops off the muffins and set them aside. Spread about ½ teaspoon of mascarpone on each muffin, then add the same amount of tapenade. Put a basil leaf on the top before replacing the muffin 'lids'.

**Note:** The tapenade can be made up to 1 week in advance and stored in an airtight container in the fridge. The muffins are best if they are made on the day they are served.

# ASIAN-FLAVOURED CRAB TARTLETS

**MAKES 30**

250 g (9 oz/2 cups) plain (all-purpose) flour

125 g (5 oz) chilled butter, chopped

1 egg

**FILLING**

60 ml (2 fl oz/¼ cup) lime juice

1 tablespoon fish sauce

1 tablespoon grated palm sugar (jaggery) or soft brown sugar

300 g (11 oz) fresh crabmeat, shredded and well drained

2 tablespoons chopped fresh coriander (cilantro) leaves

1 tablespoon chopped fresh Vietnamese mint

1 small fresh red chilli, finely chopped

2 makrut (kaffir lime) leaves, finely shredded

**1** **Preheat the oven** to 200°C (400°F/Gas 6). Lightly grease 30 mini muffin holes. Sift the flour into a bowl and rub the butter in with your fingertips until the mixture resembles fine breadcrumbs. Make a well in the centre, add the egg and mix with a flat-bladed knife, using a cutting action until it comes together in beads. If the dough seems too dry, add a little cold water. Press the dough into a ball on a lightly floured surface, then wrap it in plastic wrap and refrigerate for 30 minutes.

**2** **Roll out the dough** between two sheets of baking paper to 2 mm (¹⁄₁₆ inch) thick and cut out 30 rounds with a 6 cm (2½ inch) cutter. Press a round into each muffin hole. Prick the bases with a fork and bake for 6–8 minutes, or until golden. If they puff up, use a clean tea towel (dish towel) to press out any air pockets. Cool.

**3** **Combine the lime** juice, fish sauce and sugar in a bowl and stir until the sugar is dissolved. Mix in the rest of the ingredients, then spoon into the prepared pastry cases and serve.

**Note:** The pastry cases can be made 2–3 days ahead and kept in an airtight container. If they go soft, crisp them in a warm (170°C/325°F/ Gas 3) oven for 5 minutes.

# MAKI ZUSHI

**MAKES 48**

250 g (9 oz) sashimi tuna

1 small Lebanese (short) cucumber

1 small avocado

8 sheets nori

330 g (11 oz/1½ cups) sushi rice or
·short-grain rice

2 tablespoons seasoned rice vinegar

3 teaspoons wasabi paste

**1   Place the rice** in a sieve and rinse under cold running water. Set aside to drain for 1 hour. Place the drained rice in a large saucepan and add 375 ml (13 fl oz/1½ cups) water. Cover and bring to the boil, then reduce the heat to very low and cook, tightly covered, for 15 minutes. Remove from the heat and leave the lid on for 10 minutes.

**2   Transfer the rice** to a large shallow bowl and drizzle with the vinegar. Fold the vinegar through the rice, tossing lightly with a large metal spoon or spatula to cool as you combine. Do not use a stirring action; it will make the rice mushy.

**3   Cut the tuna,** cucumber and avocado into thin strips. Place a sheet of nori on a bamboo mat, shiny-side-down, with a short end towards you. (Bamboo mats are available at Asian grocery stores.) Spread rice about 1 cm (½ inch) thick over the nori, leaving a 1 cm (½ inch) border. Make a shallow groove down the centre of the rice towards the short end closest to you. Spread a small amount of wasabi along the groove.

**4   Place a selection** of strips of the filling ingredients on top of the wasabi. Lift up the edge of the bamboo mat and roll the sushi, starting from the edge nearest to you. When you have finished rolling, press the mat to make either a round or square roll. Push in any rice that is escaping from the ends. Then wet a sharp knife, trim the ends of the roll, cut the roll in half and then cut each half into three even pieces. Repeat with the rest of the nori, rice and filling. Refrigerate until ready to serve.

# LAYERED SUSHI

MAKES 36

90 g (3 oz/⅓ cup) Japanese mayonnaise

2 teaspoons wasabi paste

4 sheets nori

prepared sushi rice (make double the quantity given on page 78)

300 g (11 oz) smoked salmon

40 g (1½ oz/¼ cup) pickled ginger slices

black sesame seeds, to garnish

**1   Combine the mayonnaise and wasabi** in a small bowl. Lay a sheet of nori, shiny-side-up, on top of a piece of baking paper on a dry tray. Entirely cover nori with about 220 g/7 oz (a loosely packed cup) of rice. Spread with wasabi mayonnaise, top with a layer of smoked salmon and some slices of pickled ginger. Place another sheet of nori on top and flatten lightly with a rolling pin. Repeat the layering twice, to form three layers, finishing with a sheet of nori, and again flattening with the rolling pin. Reserve the remaining wasabi mayonnaise.

**2   Cover and refrigerate** for at least an hour, then, using a very sharp knife dipped in water, trim any filling protruding from the edges and slice into 2 cm (¾ inch) squares. Garnish with wasabi mayonnaise, pickled ginger and black sesame seeds. Refrigerate until ready to serve

# PRAWN SUSHI CONES

### MAKES 16

330 g (11 cups/1½ cups) sushi rice or short-grain rice

2 tablespoons seasoned rice vinegar

1 avocado

1 small Lebanese (short) cucumber

8 sheets nori, cut in half on the diagonal

1 teaspoon wasabi paste

80 g (3 oz) pickled ginger

16 cooked medium prawns (shrimp), peeled and deveined

soy sauce, to serve

1  **Place the rice** in a sieve and rinse under cold running water. Set aside to drain for 1 hour. Place the drained rice in a large saucepan and add 375 ml (13 fl oz/1½ cups) water. Cover and bring to the boil, then reduce the heat to very low and cook, tightly covered, for 15 minutes. Remove from the heat and leave the lid on for 10 minutes.

2  **Transfer the rice** to a large shallow bowl and drizzle with the vinegar. Fold the vinegar through the rice, tossing lightly with a large metal spoon or spatula to cool as you combine. Do not use a stirring action; it will make the rice mushy.

3  **Quarter and peel** the avocado and cut each quarter into four long wedges. Trim the ends of the cucumber, then cut lengthways into 16 strips.

4  **Hold a sheet of nori** shiny-side-down, flat in your hand. Place 2 tablespoons of rice on the left-hand side and spread out over half the nori sheet. Dab with a little wasabi and top with some pickled ginger. Place a strip each of avocado and cucumber on the rice and top with one prawn. Roll up the nori to form a cone, enclosing the smaller end. Repeat, using all the ingredients. Serve with soy sauce.

# VIETNAMESE RICE PAPER ROLLS

**MAKES 48**

### NUOC CHAM DIPPING SAUCE

185 ml (6 fl oz/¾ cup) fish sauce

60 ml (2 fl oz/¼ cup) lime juice

2 tablespoons grated palm sugar (jaggery) or soft brown sugar

2 bird's eye chillies, seeded and finely chopped

150 g (6 oz) dried rice vermicelli

48 round 15 cm (6 in) rice paper wrappers

48 cooked king prawns (shrimp), peeled, deveined and halved lengthways

150 g (6 oz) bean sprouts

3 large handfuls fresh mint

3 large fresh coriander (cilantro) leaves

**1** **To make the dipping sauce**, combine all the ingredients and 125 ml (4 fl oz/½ cup) water and stir until the sugar dissolves. Transfer to two small serving dishes and set aside.

**2** **Place the noodles** in a heatproof bowl, cover with boiling water and soak for 10 minutes, then drain.

**3** **Assemble the rolls** one at a time. Dip a rice paper wrapper in a bowl of warm water for 30 seconds, or until it softens. Place the wrapper on a work surface and put 2 prawn halves on the bottom third of the wrapper. Top with a few noodles, bean sprouts, mint leaves and 6 coriander leaves, in that order. Ensure that the filling is neat and compact, then turn up the bottom of the wrapper to cover the filling. Holding the filling in place, fold in the two sides, then roll up.

**4** **Arrange on a platter**, folded-side-down. Cover with a damp tea towel (dish towel) or plastic wrap until ready to serve. Serve with the dipping sauce.

Note: You can make the rolls up to 8 hours beforehand, but make sure you cover them well or they will dry out rapidly. The sauce can be made a day early.

# THAI BEEF SALAD RICE PAPER ROLLS

MAKES 16

DIPPING SAUCE

60 ml (2 fl oz/¼ cup) Japanese
    soy sauce

1 tablespoon rice vinegar

1 teaspoon sesame oil

1 tablespoon mirin

2 teaspoons fresh ginger cut into thin
    matchsticks

80 ml (3 fl oz/⅓ cup) kecap manis

80 ml (3 fl oz/⅓ cup) lime juice

1 tablespoon sesame oil

2 small red chillies, finely chopped

300 g (11 oz) piece beef eye fillet

1 stem lemon grass, white part only,
    finely chopped

60 ml (2 fl oz/¼ cup) lime juice, extra

3 tablespoons finely chopped mint

3 tablespoons finely chopped coriander
    (cilantro) leaves

1½ tablespoons fish sauce

16 square (approx. 15 cm/6 inch) rice
    paper wrappers

**1   To make the dipping sauce**, place the Japanese soy sauce, rice vinegar, sesame oil, mirin and ginger in a small bowl and mix together well.

**2   Mix the kecap manis**, lime juice, sesame oil and half the chilli in a large bowl. Add the beef and toss well to ensure all the beef is coated. Cover with plastic wrap and refrigerate for 2 hours.

**3   Heat a barbecue** or chargrill plate over high heat and cook the beef for 2–3 minutes each side, or until cooked to your liking. Cool, then slice into thin strips, against the grain.

**4   Combine the beef** with the lemon grass, extra lime juice, chopped mint, coriander, fish sauce and remaining chilli, then toss well.

**5   Dip one rice paper** wrapper at a time in warm water for a few seconds until softened. Drain, then place on a flat surface. Place a tablespoon of the mixture in the centre of the rice paper wrapper and roll up, tucking in the edges. Repeat with the remaining ingredients to make 16 rolls in total. Serve with the dipping sauce.

# PRAWN SAN CHOY BAU

### SERVES 4–6

1 large cos lettuce

1 kg (2 lb 4 oz) raw medium prawns (shrimp), peeled and deveined, or 500 g (1 lb 2 oz) raw prawn meat

1 tablespoon oil

1 teaspoon sesame oil

2 spring onions (scallions), finely chopped

2 garlic cloves, crushed

1 cm x 2 cm piece fresh ginger, peeled and grated

120 g (4 oz) drained water chestnuts, chopped

1 tablespoon chopped red chilli

185 g (7 oz/1 cup) cooked white rice

90 g (3 oz/1 cup) bean sprouts, trimmed

25 g (1 oz/½ cup) chopped coriander leaves

2 tablespoons soy sauce

2 tablespoons oyster sauce

2 tablespoons lime juice

60 ml (2 fl oz/¼ cup) hoisin sauce

**1**  **Wash the lettuce** and separate the leaves. Shake off any excess water and drain on paper towels.

**2**  **If the prawns** are large, cut them into smaller pieces. Heat a wok over high heat, add the oils, swirl to coat, then add the spring onion, crushed garlic and ginger. Cook 30 seconds then add the prawn meat, water chestnuts and chilli, season with salt and cracked black pepper, and continue stir-frying for 2 minutes. Add the cooked rice, sprouts and coriander and stir until combined.

**3**  **Add the soy sauce**, oyster sauce and lime juice, then remove from the heat. Transfer the mixture to a serving bowl. Place the dry lettuce cups on a plate and spoon the prawn mixture into each one. Serve with hoisin sauce.

# HOT FINGERFOOD

# STUFFED BLACK OLIVES

**MAKES 36**

36 pitted jumbo black or large Kalamata olives (see Note)

100 g (4 oz) goat's cheese

1 teaspoon capers, drained and finely chopped

1 garlic clove, crushed

1 tablespoon chopped flat-leaf (Italian) parsley

1½ tablespoons plain (all-purpose) flour

2 eggs, lightly beaten

100 g (4 oz/1 cup) dry breadcrumbs

1 tablespoon finely chopped flat-leaf (Italian) parsley, extra

oil, for deep-frying

lemon wedges, to serve

**1   Carefully cut the olives** along the open cavity so they are opened out, but still in one piece.

**2   Mash the goat's cheese**, capers, garlic and parsley together in a small bowl, then season. Push an even amount of the mixture into the cavity of each olive, then press them closed.

**3   Put the flour** in one small bowl, the egg in another and combine the breadcrumbs and extra parsley in a third. Dip each olive first into the flour, then into the egg and, finally, into the breadcrumbs. Put the crumbed olives on a plate and refrigerate for at least 2 hours.

**4   Fill a deep** heavy-based saucepan or deep-fryer one-third full of oil and heat to 180°C (350°F), or until a cube of bread dropped into the oil browns in 15 seconds. Cook the olives in batches for 1–2 minutes, or until golden brown all over; you may need to turn them with tongs or a long-handled metal spoon. Drain on crumpled paper towels and season. Serve warm or at room temperature with lemon wedges.

Note: If you can't find large pitted olives, buy stuffed ones and remove the filling.

# STUFFED MUSHROOMS

## SERVES 8

8 large cap mushrooms

40 g (1½ oz) butter

6 spring onions (scallions), chopped

3 garlic cloves, crushed

200 g (7 oz/2 cups) day-old breadcrumbs

1½ tablespoons finely chopped oregano

2 tablespoons chopped flat-leaf (Italian) parsley

50 g (2 oz/½ cup) grated parmesan cheese

1 egg, lightly beaten

olive oil, for greasing and drizzling

**1** **Preheat the oven** to 200°C (400°F/ Gas 6). Remove the stems from the mushrooms and discard. Wipe over the caps with a clean, damp cloth to remove any dirt.

**2** **Melt the butter** in a small frying pan over medium heat, add the spring onion and cook for 2 minutes, or until soft. Add the crushed garlic and cook for another minute. Place the breadcrumbs in a bowl and pour in the spring onion mixture, then add the herbs, parmesan and beaten egg. Season with salt and freshly cracked black pepper and mix together well.

**3** **Lightly grease a** baking tray. Divide the stuffing evenly among the mushrooms, pressing down lightly. Arrange the mushrooms on the tray, drizzle with olive oil and bake in the oven for 15 minutes, or until the tops are golden and the mushrooms are cooked through and tender.

# CAULIFLOWER FRITTERS

SERVES 4–6

600 g (1 lb 5 oz) cauliflower

55 g (2 oz/½ cup) besan (chickpea flour)

2 teaspoons ground cumin

1 teaspoon ground coriander

1 teaspoon ground turmeric

pinch cayenne pepper

1 egg, lightly beaten

1 egg yolk

oil, for deep-frying

**1** **Cut the cauliflower** into bite-sized florets. Sift the flour and spices into a bowl, then stir in ½ teaspoon salt.

**2** **Lightly whisk the** beaten egg, egg yolk and 60 ml (2 fl oz/¼ cup) water in a jug. Make a well in the centre of the dry ingredients and pour in the egg mixture, whisking until smooth. Stand for 30 minutes.

**3** **Fill a deep saucepan** one-third full of oil and heat to 180°C (350°F), or until a cube of bread dropped into the oil browns in 15 seconds. Dip the florets into the batter, allowing the excess to drain into the bowl. Deep-fry in batches for about 3 minutes per batch, or until puffed and browned. Drain, sprinkle with salt and extra cayenne, if desired, and serve hot.

# SPINACH AND LEEK FRITTERS

**MAKES 8**

| |
|---|
| 40 g (1½ oz) butter |
| 40 g (1½ oz/¼ cup) pine nuts |
| 1 leek, white part only, thinly sliced |
| 100 g (3½ oz) baby English spinach, chopped |
| 3 eggs |
| 1 egg yolk |
| 1 tablespoon cream |
| 75 g (¾ cup) grated parmesan cheese |
| 1 tablespoon chopped parsley |
| 1 tablespoon olive oil |

**1**  **Melt half the butter** in a heavy-based frying pan over low–medium heat and cook the pine nuts and leek for 3 minutes, or until the pine nuts are golden. Add the spinach and cook for 1 minute. Remove the mixture from the pan and allow to cool slightly. Wipe out the pan with paper towels.

**2**  **Whisk the eggs,** yolk and cream together in a large bowl. Add the cheese and parsley and season with salt and freshly ground black pepper. Stir in the spinach mixture.

**3**  **Melt half of the remaining butter** and half of the oil in the frying pan. Place four 5–7 cm (2–2¾ inch) egg rings in the pan, and pour 60 ml (2 fl oz/¼ cup) of the spinach mixture into each. Cook over low heat for 2–3 minutes, or until the base is set. Gently flip and cook the other side for 2–3 minutes, or until firm. Transfer to a plate and slide out of the egg rings. Repeat with the remaining butter, oil and spinach mixture.

# SCALLOPS ON POTATO CRISPS WITH PEA PURÉE

**MAKES 48**

1 tablespoon butter

3 French shallots, finely chopped

1 garlic clove, finely chopped

2 slices mild pancetta, finely chopped

155 g (6 oz/1 cup) frozen peas

60 ml (2 fl oz/¼ cup) chicken stock
  or water

oil, for deep-frying, plus 1 tablespoon

4–5 floury potatoes (e.g. russet, king
  edward), peeled and very thinly sliced
  to get 48 slices

24 scallops, cut in half horizontally
  through the centre

fresh mint, to garnish

**1**  **Melt the butter** in a small saucepan and fry the shallots, garlic and pancetta over low heat for 3 minutes, or until soft but not coloured. Add the peas and stock, and cook over high heat for 3 minutes, or until all the liquid has evaporated. Cool a little, transfer to a food processor and purée until smooth. Season.

**2**  **Fill a deep** heavy-based saucepan or deep-fryer one-third full of oil and heat to 190°C (375°F), or until a cube of bread dropped into the oil browns in 10 seconds. Cook the potato slices in batches until crisp and golden. Drain on crumpled paper towels and sprinkle with salt.

**3**  **Toss the scallops** with 1 tablespoon oil. Season lightly. Heat a chargrill pan to hot, then sear the scallops in batches for 5 seconds each side, or until lightly browned on the outside but opaque in the middle.

**4**  **Reheat the pea purée.** Dollop 1 teaspoon of purée on each potato crisp, then top with a scallop. Season with pepper and garnish with mint.

**Note:** Purée can be made 2 days early and refrigerated. Crisps can be cooked 2 hours early; store in an airtight container.

# STEAMED SCALLOPS WITH LIME SAUCE

**SERVES 4 AS A STARTER**

LIME SAUCE

1 teaspoon soft brown sugar

2 tablespoons lime juice

¼ teaspoon chilli sauce

1 tablespoon sweet soy sauce

12 scallops in the half shell

2 small makrut (kaffir lime) leaves, shredded

12 Thai basil or holy basil leaves, torn

1 small red chilli, seeded and thinly sliced

**1** **To make the lime sauce,** combine the sugar, lime juice, chilli sauce and sweet soy sauce in a small bowl.

**2** **Fill a large wok** one-third full of water, bring to the boil then reduce to a simmer. Cover with a bamboo steamer and arrange four scallops in their shells in the steamer. Cover and steam for 2–3 minutes, or until the scallops are opaque but still plump (the time will depend on their plumpness). Remove with tongs and steam the remaining scallops. As each batch is taken out, add the juices from the shells to the lime sauce.

**3** **Arrange three shells** on each serving plate. Spoon a little sauce over the scallops and top with the lime and basil leaves and the chilli. Serve warm or chilled.

# DEEP-FRIED OYSTERS WITH THAI DIPPING SAUCE

**SERVES 4 AS A SIDE DISH**

24 Pacific oysters or any other large
   oyster on the shell

30 g (1 oz/¼ cup) plain (all-purpose)
   flour

1 egg, mixed with 3 teaspoons
   cold water

60 g (2 oz/1 cup) panko (Japanese
   breadcrumbs) or dry packaged
   breadcrumbs

vegetable oil, for deep-frying

**SWEET THAI DIPPING SAUCE**

4 tablespoons white wine vinegar

2½ tablespoons caster (superfine) sugar

1 slice fresh ginger

1 Lebanese (short) cucumber, seeded
   and finely diced

1 small red chilli, seeded and sliced

1 tablespoon chopped coriander
   (cilantro) leaves

**1  Remove the oysters** from their shells and lightly coat in the flour. Wash the shells, removing any grit from them, then dry well and set aside for later. Coat oysters in the egg mixture and then the panko, pressing on firmly. Arrange oysters on a plate, cover and refrigerate for at least 30 minutes.

**2  To make dipping sauce,** put the vinegar, sugar and ginger in a small saucepan and heat to dissolve the sugar. Bring to the boil, then remove from the heat and allow to cool to room temperature. Discard the ginger and stir in the cucumber, chilli and coriander.

**3  Fill a wok** one-third full of oil to 180°C (350°F), or until a cube of bread dropped in the oil browns in 15 seconds. Deep-fry the oysters in batches for 1 minute, or until golden brown. Remove from the oil with a slotted spoon and drain on crumpled paper towels. Put the oysters back in the shells and drizzle with the dipping sauce or, if you prefer, serve the sauce in a bowl on the side.

# STEAMED OYSTERS WITH HOT SESAME OIL

**MAKES 24**

rock salt, for lining

24 shucked oysters

3 spring onions (scallions), trimmed and cut into thin matchsticks

1 long red chilli, seeded and cut into very thin strips

3 teaspoons finely grated fresh ginger

1 tablespoon light soy sauce

1 tablespoon roughly chopped coriander (cilantro) leaves (optional)

1 tablespoon sesame oil

**1** **Fill a wok** one-third full of water; bring to simmering point. Take a plate that fits in the steamer basket (with sufficient space around it for you to remove the plate when it is hot) and line the plate with rock salt.

**2** **Arrange a single layer** of oysters on top of the salt — this will prevent them sliding around. Put some spring onion, chilli and ginger on each oyster and drizzle with a little soy sauce. Cover; steam over the wok of simmering water for 2 minutes. Repeat with remaining oysters, scattering with a little coriander when steamed.

**3** **Put the sesame oil** in a small saucepan and heat briefly over high heat. Drizzle oil over the oysters and serve at once.

# WHITEBAIT FRITTERS WITH TARTARE SAUCE

**MAKES 50**

125 g (5 oz/1 cup) plain (all-purpose) flour

1 large egg, lightly beaten

250 ml (9 fl oz/1 cup) iced water

3 tablespoons chopped parsley

3 teaspoons grated lemon zest

400 g (14 oz) whitebait

oil, for deep-frying

**TARTARE SAUCE**

2 egg yolks

1 teaspoon dijon mustard

250 ml (9 fl oz/1 cup) olive oil

1 tablespoon lemon juice

2 tablespoons capers, drained and chopped

2 tablespoons chopped gherkins (pickle)

1 tablespoon chopped fresh parsley

1 tablespoon chopped fresh tarragon

**1**  **Sift the flour** and a pinch of salt and pepper into a large bowl, make a well in the centre and add the egg. Whisk gently and gradually add the water, stirring constantly to a smooth batter. Stir in the parsley and lemon zest. Refrigerate, covered, for 1 hour.

**2**  **To make the tartare sauce,** place the egg yolks and mustard in a food processor and pulse for 10 seconds. With the motor running, slowly add the oil in a thin stream until the mixture is thick and creamy. Add lemon juice and 2 teaspoons boiling water and pulse for another 10 seconds. Transfer to a bowl, add capers, gherkins, parsley and tarragon and season generously. Cover and refrigerate until needed.

**3**  **Pat the whitebait dry,** then gently stir into the batter. Fill a large heavy-based saucepan one-third full of oil and heat to 190°C (375°F), or until a cube of bread dropped in the oil browns in 10 seconds. Put small tablespoons of batter into the oil. Cook the fritters in batches, gently tossing in the oil. Cook for 2 minutes, or until the fritters are golden brown. Drain on crumpled paper towels; keep warm. Repeat with the remaining mixture. Serve immediately with the tartare sauce.

# PRAWN TOASTS

MAKES 36

DIPPING SAUCE

125 ml (5 oz/½ cup) tomato sauce

2 garlic cloves, crushed

2 small red chillies, seeded and finely chopped

2 tablespoons hoisin sauce

2 teaspoons worcestershire sauce

350 g (12 oz) raw medium prawns (shrimp)

1 garlic clove

75 g (3 oz) tinned water chestnuts, drained

1 tablespoon chopped coriander (cilantro)

2.5 cm (1 inch) piece fresh ginger, roughly chopped

2 eggs, separated

¼ teaspoon white pepper

12 slices white bread, crusts removed

155 g (6 oz/1 cup) sesame seeds

oil, for deep-frying

**1  To make the dipping sauce**, combine all the ingredients in a small bowl.

**2  Peel the prawns** and gently pull out the dark vein from each prawn back, starting at the head end. Put the prawns in a food processor with the garlic, water chestnuts, coriander, ginger, egg whites, pepper and ¼ teaspoon salt and process for 20–30 seconds, or until smooth.

**3  Brush the top** of each slice of bread with lightly beaten egg yolk, then spread evenly with the prawn mixture. Sprinkle generously with sesame seeds. Cut each slice of bread into three even strips.

**4  Fill a large** heavy-based saucepan one-third full of oil and heat to 180°C (350°F), or until a cube of bread browns in 15 seconds. Deep-fry the toasts in batches for 10–15 seconds, or until golden and crisp. Start with the prawn mixture face down, then turn halfway. Remove the toasts from the oil with tongs or a slotted spoon and drain on crumpled paper towels. Serve with the dipping sauce.

**Note:** The uncooked prawn toasts can be frozen for up to 1 month. Allow them to thaw slightly before deep-frying.

# DRESSED-UP BABY POTATOES

**MAKES 24**

24 even bite-sized new potatoes, washed and dried

80 ml (3 fl oz/⅓ cup) olive oil

1 tablespoon drained capers, patted dry

1 slice bacon

1 tablespoon cream

10 g (½ oz) butter

125 g (5 oz/½ cup) sour cream

1 tablespoon snipped chives

1 tablespoon red or black fish roe

**1**   **Preheat the oven** to 180°C (350°F/Gas 4). Line a baking tray with baking paper. Place the potatoes in a bowl and toss with half the olive oil. Sprinkle with salt and freshly ground black pepper. Place on the baking tray; bake for 40 minutes, or until cooked through, rotating them 2–3 times so that they brown evenly.

**2**   **Meanwhile, heat the remaining oil** in a frying pan and cook the capers over high heat, or until they open into small flowers. Drain on paper towels. Cook the bacon under a hot grill (broiler) until crisp. Cool, then finely chop.

**3**   **Remove the potatoes** from the oven. When cool enough to handle, cut a thin lid from each potato. Discard the lids. Use a melon baller or small teaspoon to scoop out the flesh from the middle of the potatoes, leaving a 1 cm (½ inch) border. Put the potato flesh in a bowl and mash thoroughly with the cream, butter and salt and freshly ground black pepper. Spoon the mash back into the potatoes.

**4**   **Top each potato** with a small dollop of sour cream. Divide the potatoes into four groups of six and use a separate topping for each group: capers, bacon, chives and fish roe.

# GOAT'S CHEESE FRITTERS WITH CAPSICUM SAUCE

**MAKES 30**

ROASTED CAPSICUM SAUCE

2 red capsicums (peppers)

2 tablespoons olive oil

1 small red onion, finely chopped

1 garlic clove

80 ml (3 fl oz/⅓ cup) chicken or
vegetable stock

420 g (15 oz) ricotta cheese, well
drained

400 g (14 oz) goat's cheese, crumbled

2 tablespoons snipped chives

30 g (1 oz/¼ cup) plain (all-purpose)
flour

2 eggs, lightly beaten

100 g (4 oz/1 cup) dry breadcrumbs

oil, for deep-frying

**1** **Cut the capsicums** into 2–3 pieces, removing the seeds and membrane. Place, skin-side-up, under a hot grill (broiler) until the skin blackens and blisters. Cool in a plastic bag, then peel away the skin and roughly chop the flesh.

**2** **Heat the olive oil** in a frying pan over medium heat and cook the onion and garlic for 5 minutes, or until softened. Add the capsicum and stock. Bring to the boil, then remove from the heat, cool slightly and transfer to a food processor. Pulse until combined, but still a little lumpy. Season and refrigerate until needed.

**3** **Combine the ricotta,** goat's cheese and chives in a bowl. Add the flour and eggs, then season and mix well.

**4** **Put the breadcrumbs** in a bowl. Roll a tablespoon of the cheese mixture into a ball with damp hands, flatten slightly and coat in the breadcrumbs. Repeat with the remaining mixture. Refrigerate for 30 minutes.

**5** **Fill a deep** heavy-based saucepan one-third full of oil and heat to 180°C (350°F), or until a cube of bread browns in 15 seconds. Cook the fritters in batches for 1 minute, or until browned, then drain. Serve warm with the capsicum sauce.

# MONEY BAGS

MAKES 30

1 tablespoon peanut oil

4 red Asian shallots, finely chopped

2 garlic cloves, crushed

1 tablespoon grated fresh ginger

150 g (6 oz) minced (ground) chicken

150 g (6 oz) minced (ground) pork

40 g (1½ oz/¼ cup) roasted peanuts, chopped

3 tablespoons finely chopped coriander (cilantro) leaves

3 teaspoons fish sauce

2 teaspoons soy sauce

2 teaspoons lime juice

2 teaspoons grated palm sugar (jaggery) or soft brown sugar

30 won ton wrappers

oil, for deep-frying

garlic chives, for tying

DIPPING SAUCE

2 teaspoons sugar

125 ml (4 fl oz/½ cup) rice wine vinegar

2 small fresh red chillies, seeded and chopped

**1** **Heat the oil** in a frying pan over medium heat. Add the shallots, garlic and ginger and cook for 1–2 minutes, or until the shallots are soft. Add the mince and cook for 4 minutes, or until cooked, breaking up any lumps with a wooden spoon. Stir in the peanuts, coriander, fish sauce, soy sauce, lime juice and sugar and cook, stirring, for 1–2 minutes, or until mixed and reduced. Cool.

**2** **Form your thumb** and index finger into a circle, and place a won ton wrapper on top. Place 2 teaspoons of the cooled mixture in the centre, then lightly brush the edges with water. Push the mixture down firmly with your free hand, tightening the circle of your thumb and index finger at the same time, encasing the mixture in the wrapper and forming a 'bag'. Trim.

**3** **Fill a deep** heavy-based saucepan or deep-fryer one-third full of oil and heat to 190°C (375°F), or until a cube of bread browns in 10 seconds. Cook in batches for 30–60 seconds, or until golden. Drain. Tie the 'neck' of the money bags with the chives.

**4** **To make the dipping sauce**, dissolve the sugar and 1 teaspoon salt in the vinegar. Add the chilli and mix. Serve with the dipping sauce.

# MINI CRAB CAKES WITH CORIANDER PASTE

**MAKES 24**

1 tablespoon butter

4 spring onions (scallions), thinly sliced

1 egg

2 tablespoons sour cream

350 g (12 oz) fresh white crabmeat,
excess liquid squeezed out

1 small yellow capsicum (pepper),
finely diced

2 teaspoons chopped thyme

200 g (7 oz/2½ cups) fresh white
breadcrumbs

olive oil, for shallow-frying

**CORIANDER PASTE**

1 garlic clove

1 green chilli, seeded

½ teaspoon ground cumin

¼ teaspoon sugar

2 large handfuls coriander (cilantro)
leaves

1 large handful fresh mint

1 tablespoon lemon juice

1 tablespoon coconut cream

1 small avocado

**1  Line a tray** with baking paper. Melt the butter in a frying pan over low heat. When it begins to foam, add the spring onion and cook for 2 minutes, or until softened. Remove from the heat and cool.

**2  Mix the egg** and sour cream until just smooth. Add the spring onion, crab, capsicum, thyme and 40g (1½ oz/½ cup) of the breadcrumbs, season and mix together. Shape the mixture into flat rounds, using 1 level tablespoon for each. Place on the tray and refrigerate for 30 minutes.

**3  Meanwhile, to make** the coriander paste, process the garlic, chilli, cumin, sugar, herbs, lemon juice and ¼ teaspoon salt in a food processor until a fine paste forms. Add the coconut cream and continue to blend until smooth. Add the avocado and, using the pulse action, process until just smooth. Transfer to a bowl, cover with plastic wrap and chill.

**4  Using your hands,** coat the crab cakes in the remaining breadcrumbs. Heat enough olive oil in a non-stick frying pan to just coat the bottom. Cook in batches for 2–3 minutes each side, or until golden. Drain and serve warm with ½ teaspoon of coriander paste on each.

# CARAMELIZED RED ONION AND FETA TARTLETS

**MAKES 24**

1½ tablespoons olive oil

2 large red onions, finely chopped

2 teaspoons chopped thyme

3 sheets ready-rolled shortcrust pastry

70 g (2 oz) feta cheese, crumbled

2 eggs, lightly beaten

125 ml (4 fl oz/½ cup) pouring cream

**1** **Preheat the oven** to 180°C (350°F/Gas 4). Heat oil in a frying pan (do not use a non-stick one or the onion won't caramelize). Add the onion and cook, stirring occasionally, over medium–low heat for 30 minutes, or until dark gold. Add the thyme, stir well and transfer to a bowl to cool.

**2** **Grease 24 shallow** mini muffin tins. Using an 7.5 cm (3 inch) cutter, cut out 24 pastry rounds and line tins with the rounds.

**3** **Divide the onion** among the muffin holes, then spoon the feta over the onion. Combine the eggs with the cream, season and pour into the pastry cases. Bake for 10–15 minutes, or until puffed and golden. Leave in the tins for 5 minutes before transferring to a wire rack to cool.

**Note:** These can be made a day in advance and reheated in a slow (150°C/300°F/Gas 2) oven for 10 minutes before serving.

# MUSHROOM RAGOUT TARTLETS

MAKES 30

**BASIC PASTRY CASES**

250 g (9 oz/2 cups) plain (all-purpose) flour

125 g (5 oz) chilled butter, chopped

1 egg

50 g (2 oz) butter

4 spring onions (scallions), chopped

2 garlic cloves, chopped

150 g (6 oz) small Swiss brown or shiitake mushrooms, thinly sliced

100 g (4 oz) oyster mushrooms, cut into eighths

50 g (2 oz) enoki mushrooms, trimmed, pulled apart and sliced lengthways

3 teaspoons plain (all-purpose) flour

2 tablespoons chicken stock or water

2 tablespoons sake

80 ml (3 fl oz/⅓ cup) thick (double/heavy) cream

snow pea (mangetout) sprouts, stalks removed

**1   Preheat the oven** to 200°C (400°F/Gas 6). Lightly grease 30 mini muffin holes. Sift the flour and rub the butter in with your fingertips until the mixture resembles fine breadcrumbs. Make a well in the centre, add the egg and mix with a flat-bladed knife, using a cutting action until it comes together in beads. If the dough seems too dry, add a little cold water. Press the dough into a ball on a lightly floured surface, then wrap it in plastic wrap and refrigerate for 30 minutes.

**2   Roll out the dough** between sheets of baking paper to 2 mm (1/16 inch) thick. Cut out 30 rounds with a 6 cm (2½ inch) cutter. Press a round into each hole. Prick the bases with a fork and bake for 8 minutes, or until golden. If they puff up, use a clean cloth to press back. Cool.

**3   Melt the butter** in a frying pan over medium heat, add the spring onion and garlic and cook for 1 minute. Add the mushrooms and cook, stirring, for 3–4 minutes, or until soft. Add the flour and stir for another minute. Pour in the stock and sake and stir for 1 minute, or until evaporated, then add the cream and cook for 1 minute, or until thickened. Season. Spoon into the prepared pastry cases and top each one with a snow pea sprout leaf.

# CRUMBED PRAWNS WITH PONZU DIPPING SAUCE

**MAKES 18**

18 raw large prawns (shrimp)

2 tablespoons cornflour (cornstarch)

3 eggs

240 g (9 oz/3 cups) fresh breadcrumbs

oil, for pan-frying

80 ml (3 fl oz/⅓ cup) ponzu sauce or 60 ml (2 fl oz/¼ cup) soy sauce with 1 tablespoon lemon juice

**1  Peel and devein** the prawns, leaving the tails intact. Cut down the back of each prawn to form a butterfly. Place each prawn between two layers of plastic wrap and gently beat to form a cutlet.

**2  Put the cornflour,** eggs and breadcrumbs in separate bowls. Lightly beat the eggs. Dip each prawn first into the cornflour then into the egg and finally into the breadcrumbs, ensuring that each cutlet is well covered in crumbs.

**3  Heat the oil** in a frying pan over medium heat until hot. Cook six prawn cutlets at a time for about 1 minute each side, or until the crumbs are golden. Be careful they don't burn. Serve immediately with ponzu sauce.

**Note:** Ponzu is a Japanese dipping sauce usually used for sashimi.

# SALT AND PEPPER SQUID

**SERVES 12**

1 kg (2 lb 4 oz) squid tubes, halved
  lengthways (see Note)

250 ml (9 fl oz/1 cup) lemon juice

125 g (5 oz/1 cup) cornflour (cornstarch)

1½ tablespoons salt

1 tablespoon ground white pepper

2 teaspoons caster (superfine) sugar

4 egg whites, lightly beaten

oil, for deep-frying

lemon wedges, for serving

**1  Open out the squid tubes,** then wash and pat dry. Lay on a chopping board with the inside facing upwards. Score a fine diamond pattern on the inside, being careful not to cut all the way through. Cut squid into pieces 5 cm x 2 cm (2 x ¾ inch). Place in a flat non-metallic dish and pour on the lemon juice. Cover and refrigerate for 15 minutes. Drain well and pat dry.

**2  Combine the cornflour,** salt, white pepper and sugar in a bowl. Dip the squid into the egg white and lightly coat with the cornflour mixture, shaking off any excess.

**3  Fill a deep** heavy-based pan or deep-fryer one-third full of oil. Heat to 180°C (350°F), or until a cube of bread dropped into the oil turns golden brown in 15 seconds. Deep-fry the squid, in batches, for 1 minute each batch, or until the squid turns lightly golden and curls up. Drain on crumpled paper towels. Serve with lemon wedges.

**Note:** If you are cleaning the squid yourself, reserve the tentacles, cut them into groups of two or three depending on the size; marinate and cook them with the tubes.

# ROAST BEEF ON CROÛTES

**MAKES 30**

300 g (11 oz) piece beef eye fillet

80 ml (3 fl oz/⅓ cup) olive oil

2 garlic cloves, crushed

2 thyme sprigs plus extra to garnish

10 slices white bread

1 large garlic clove, peeled, extra

**HORSERADISH CREAM**

80 ml (3 fl oz/⅓ cup) thick (double/ heavy) cream

1 tablespoon grated horseradish (see Note)

1 teaspoon lemon juice

**1** **Place the beef** in a non-metallic bowl, pour on the combined oil, garlic and thyme and toss to coat well. Cover with plastic wrap and marinate in the refrigerator for about 3 hours. Preheat the oven to 200°C (400°F/Gas 6).

**2** **To make the croûtes,** cut out three rounds from each slice of bread using a 5 cm (2 inch) fluted cutter. Place the rounds on a baking tray and bake for 5 minutes each side, then rub the whole garlic clove over each side of the rounds and set aside.

**3** **To make the horseradish cream,** put the cream in a small bowl and whisk lightly until thickened. Gently fold in the horseradish and lemon juice, then season with cracked black pepper. Refrigerate until ready to use.

**4** **Heat a roasting tin** in the oven for 5 minutes. Remove the beef from the marinade, reserving the marinade. Generously season the beef on all sides with salt and pepper, then place it in the hot roasting tin and turn it so that all sides of the meat are sealed. Drizzle with 2 tablespoons of the reserved marinade, then roast for 10–12 minutes for rare, or until cooked to your liking. Remove from the oven, cover with foil and leave to rest for 15 minutes before slicing thinly.

**5** **Arrange one slice** of beef on each croûte (you may need to cut the slices in half if too big), top with ½ teaspoon of the horseradish cream and a small sprig of fresh thyme.

**Note:** Grated horseradish is available in small jars preserved in vinegar. Don't confuse it with horseradish sauce, which already has a cream base.

# ZUCCHINI AND HALOUMI FRITTERS

**MAKES 45**

300 g (11 oz) zucchini (courgette)

4 spring onions (scallions), thinly sliced

200 g (7 oz) haloumi cheese, coarsely grated

30 g (1 oz/¼ cup) plain (all-purpose) flour

2 eggs

1 tablespoon chopped fresh dill, plus sprigs, to garnish

60 ml (2 fl oz/¼ cup) oil

1 lemon, cut into very thin slices, seeds removed

90 g (3 oz/⅓ cup) thick Greek-style yoghurt

**1** **Coarsely grate the zucchini** and squeeze out as much liquid as possible in your hands or in a clean tea towel. Combine the zucchini with the spring onion, haloumi, flour, eggs and dill. Season well with salt and cracked black pepper.

**2** **Heat the oil** in a large heavy-based frying pan. Form fritters (using heaped teaspoons of the mixture) and cook in batches for 2 minutes each side, or until golden and firm. Drain on crumpled paper towels.

**3** **Cut each lemon** slice into quarters or eighths, depending on their size, to make small triangles.

**4** **Top each fritter** with ½ teaspoon yoghurt, a piece of lemon and a small sprig of dill.

Note: The fritters are best prepared and cooked as close to serving time as possible or the haloumi tends to toughen.

# GYOZA

**MAKES 45**

300 g (11 oz) minced (ground) pork

250 g (9 oz) finely shredded and lightly blanched Chinese cabbage with the excess water squeezed out

60 g snipped Chinese chives

1 tablespoon finely chopped fresh ginger

60 ml (2 fl oz/¼ cup) soy sauce

1 tablespoon rice wine

1 teaspoon sugar

45 gow gee wrappers

2 teaspoons oil

## DIPPING SAUCE

2 tablespoons soy sauce

1 tablespoon black Chinese vinegar

1 teaspoon sesame oil

½ teaspoon chilli oil

**1  Combine the pork** mince, Chinese cabbage, Chinese chives and ginger in a bowl. Add the soy sauce, rice wine, sugar and 1 teaspoon salt and mix together very well.

**2  Place a gow gee wrapper** flat in the palm of your hand, then place 2 teaspoons of the filling mixture into the centre of the wrapper. With wet fingers, bring the sides together to form a half-moon shape and pinch the seam firmly to seal it in a pleat.

**3  Press one side** of the dumplings onto a flat surface to create a flat bottom; this will make it easier to pan-fry them.

**4  Heat the oil** in a frying pan over medium–high heat. Add the gyoza to the pan in batches and cook for 1–2 minutes on the flat side, without moving, so that the gyoza become brown and crisp on that side. Transfer to a plate. Return the gyoza to the pan in batches. Gradually add 100 ml (4 fl oz) water to the pan. Cover and steam for 5 minutes. Empty the pan and wipe it dry between batches.

**5  To make the dipping sauce,** combine all the ingredients in a small bowl. Serve with the gyoza.

# HONEY PRAWNS

**MAKES 16**

| |
|---|
| 16 raw large prawns (shrimp) |
| cornflour (cornstarch), for dusting |
| oil, for deep-frying |
| 3 egg whites, lightly beaten |
| 2 tablespoons cornflour, extra |
| 2 tablespoons oil, extra |
| 90 g (3 oz/¼ cup) honey |
| 2 tablespoons sesame seeds, toasted |

**1  Peel and devein** the prawns, leaving the tails intact. Pat them dry and lightly dust with the cornflour, shaking off any excess. Fill a large heavy-based saucepan or wok one-third full of oil and heat to 180°C (350°F), or until a cube of bread dropped in the oil browns in 15 seconds.

**2  Beat the egg whites** in a clean dry bowl until soft peaks form. Add the extra cornflour and some salt and gently whisk until combined and smooth. Using the tail as a handle, dip the prawns in the batter, then slowly lower them into the oil. Cook in batches for 3–4 minutes, or until crisp and golden and the prawns are cooked. Remove with a slotted spoon, then drain on crumpled paper towels and keep warm.

**3  Heat the extra** oil and honey in a saucepan over medium heat for 2–3 minutes, or until bubbling. Place the prawns on a serving plate and pour on the honey sauce. Sprinkle with the sesame seeds and serve immediately.

# SPICY CORN PUFFS

**MAKES ABOUT 36**

2 corn cobs

3 tablespoons chopped coriander (cilantro) leaves

6 spring onions (scallions), finely chopped

1 small red chilli, seeded and finely chopped

1 large egg

2 teaspoons ground cumin

½ teaspoon ground coriander

125 g (5 oz/1 cup) plain (all-purpose) flour

oil, for deep-frying

sweet chilli sauce, to serve

**1** **Cut down the** side of the corn with a sharp knife to release the kernels. Roughly chop the kernels, then place them in a large bowl. Holding the cobs over the bowl, scrape down the sides of the cobs with a knife to release any corn juice from the cob into the bowl.

**2** **Add the fresh** coriander, spring onion, chilli, egg, cumin, ground coriander, 1 teaspoon salt and some cracked black pepper to the bowl and stir well. Add the flour and mix well.

**3** **The texture of the batter** will vary depending on the juiciness of the corn. If the mixture is too dry, add 1 tablespoon water, but no more than that as the batter should be quite dry. Stand for 10 minutes.

**4** **Fill a large** heavy-based saucepan or deep-fryer one-third full of oil and heat to 180°C (350°F), or until a cube of bread dropped in the oil browns in 15 seconds. Drop slightly heaped teaspoons of the corn batter into the oil and cook for about 1½ minutes, or until puffed and golden. Drain on crumpled paper towels and serve immediately with a bowl of the sweet chilli sauce to dip the puffs into.

**Note:** The corn puffs should be prepared just before serving.

# TURKISH BREAD WITH HERBED ZUCCHINI

**MAKES 48**

½ large loaf Turkish (flat) bread
1 tablespoon sesame seeds
125 ml (4 fl oz/½ cup) vegetable oil

**HERBED ZUCCHINI**

1 tablespoon olive oil
2 garlic cloves, finely chopped
4 x 100 g (4 oz) small zucchini (courgettes), roughly chopped
1 large carrot, thinly sliced
2 tablespoons chopped flat-leaf (Italian) parsley
2 tablespoons chopped mint
2 teaspoons lemon juice
½ teaspoon ground cumin

**1  Split the bread** horizontally through the middle and open it out. Cut the bread into 2.5 cm (1 inch) squares; you should end up with 48 squares.

**2  Toast the sesame seeds** in a large dry non-stick frying pan over low heat for 2–3 minutes, or until golden. Remove from the pan. Heat the vegetable oil in the same pan and cook the bread in batches for 1–2 minutes each side, or until crisp and golden. Drain on paper towels.

**3  Heat the olive oil** in a saucepan over medium heat and cook the garlic for 1 minute. Add the zucchini and carrot and cook over medium heat for 2 minutes. Season with salt and pepper. Add 1 tablespoon water, cover and simmer over low heat for 15 minutes, or until the vegetables are soft. Spoon into a bowl and mash roughly with a potato masher. Add the parsley, mint, lemon juice and cumin. Season to taste.

**4  Spoon 2 teaspoons** of the zucchini mixture over each square of bread and scatter with sesame seeds. Serve warm or at room temperature.

**Note:** The herbed zucchini can be prepared up to 2 days in advance. Reheat just before serving.

# PRAWN POTSTICKERS

**MAKES 24**

DIPPING SAUCE

60 ml (2 fl oz/¼ cup) soy sauce

1 spring onion (scallion), thinly sliced

1 garlic clove, crushed

¼ teaspoon finely chopped fresh ginger

¼ teaspoon sesame oil

500 g (1 lb 2 oz) raw medium prawns
    (shrimp)

40 g (1½ oz) Chinese cabbage, finely
    shredded

40 g (1½ oz) drained water chestnuts,
    finely chopped

1 tablespoon finely chopped coriander
    (cilantro) leaves

24 round gow gee wrappers (see Note)

1 tablespoon vegetable oil

125 ml (4 fl oz/½ cup) chicken stock

**1**  **To make the dipping sauce,** combine all the ingredients in a small bowl.

**2**  **Peel and devein** the prawns, then finely chop. Combine the prawn meat, cabbage, water chestnuts and coriander.

**3**  **Lay all the gow gee wrappers** out on a work surface and put one heaped teaspoon of the prawn filling in the centre of each. Moisten the edges with water and draw together into the shape of a moneybag, pressing the edges together firmly to seal.

**4**  **Heat the oil** in a large frying pan and add the potstickers. Cook in batches over medium heat for 2 minutes, or until just brown on the bottom. Add the stock, then quickly cover with a lid as it will spit. Steam for 2–3 minutes, taking care that all the stock does not evaporate and the potstickers do not burn. Serve immediately with the dipping sauce.

Note: Gow gee wrappers are rolled–out round pieces of dough made from wheat flour and water. They are available from Asian food stores.

# SPRING ROLLS

**MAKES 30**

50 g (2 oz) mung bean vermicelli

1 tablespoon oil

2 large garlic cloves, crushed

2 tablespoons grated fresh ginger

6 spring onions (scallions), chopped

4 coriander (cilantro) roots, finely chopped

200 g (7 oz) peeled raw prawns (shrimp), minced

200 g (7 oz) minced (ground) pork

125 g (5 oz) grated carrot

3 tablespoons finely chopped coriander (cilantro) leaves

2 tablespoons sweet chilli sauce

1 tablespoon fish sauce

2 tablespoons soy sauce

30 small spring roll wrappers

1 egg white, lightly beaten

oil, extra, for deep-frying

**1   Soak the vermicelli** in warm water for 5 minutes. Drain and cut into short lengths.

**2   Heat the oil** in a large saucepan over medium heat. Add garlic, ginger, spring onion and coriander root and cook for 1–2 minutes, or until soft. Add the prawn and pork mince and cook, until cooked through, breaking up the lumps. Stir in the vermicelli, carrot and coriander leaves. Cook for 1 minute. Add the sweet chilli, fish and soy sauces and cook for a further 2 minutes, or until dry. Cool.

**3   Place a tablespoon** of the mixture along the centre of each spring roll wrapper. Brush the edge with egg white and roll up, tucking in the ends as you go. Cover to prevent drying.

**4   Fill a deep heavy-based** saucepan one-third full of oil and heat to 190°C (375°F), or until a cube of bread browns in 10 seconds. Cook the rolls in batches for 30–60 seconds, or until golden. Remove with a slotted spoon and drain on paper towels.

# BETEL AND TOFU BITES

**MAKES 24**

2 tablespoons brown sugar

24 betel leaves or large basil leaves

1 tablespoon oil

2 garlic cloves, crushed

1 tablespoon grated fresh ginger

2 small red chillies, seeded and finely chopped

200 g (7 oz) fried tofu puffs, shredded

2 fresh makrut (kaffir lime) leaves, finely shredded

3 tablespoons lime juice

2 tablespoons shaved palm sugar (jaggery) or soft brown sugar

3 tablespoons coriander (cilantro) leaves

2 tablespoons desiccated coconut, toasted

**1**   **In a bowl,** combine the sugar and 500 ml (17 fl oz/2 cups) water. Stir in the betel leaves, soak for 10 minutes, then drain.

**2**   **Heat the oil** in a frying pan and cook the garlic, ginger and chilli over medium heat for 1 minute.

**3**   **Add the tofu,** lime leaves and the combined lime juice, palm sugar and coriander. Stir until the tofu is heated through.

**4**   **Place 1 tablespoon** of tofu mixture onto each betel leaf and lightly sprinkle with coconut. To eat, roll the leaf around the filling to contain it.

# SEARED SALMON

## SERVES 4–6

600 g (1 lb 5 oz) salmon fillet

1 tablespoon cracked black pepper

1 teaspoon sea salt

2 tablespoons olive oil

### SPICY COCKTAIL SAUCE

185 g (7 oz/¾ cup) whole-egg mayonnaise

3 tablespoons tomato sauce

2 teaspoons worcestershire sauce

1 teaspoon lemon juice

1 teaspoon sweet chilli sauce

2 teaspoons chopped flat-leaf (Italian) parsley

**1** **Remove the skin** and bones from the salmon fillet and cut into 2.5 cm (1 inch) cubes. Toss cubes in the combined black pepper and sea salt. Heat the olive oil in a large frying pan and brown the salmon over high heat. Insert a toothpick in each piece and serve with the cocktail sauce.

**2** **To make the sauce**, stir together the mayonnaise, tomato sauce, worcestershire sauce, lemon juice, sweet chilli sauce and parsley in a bowl.

# TOFU AND VEGETABLE KOFTAS WITH YOGHURT SAUCE

SERVES 4

YOGHURT DIPPING SAUCE

200 g (7 oz) plain soy yoghurt

1 garlic clove, crushed

2 tablespoons fresh mint, finely chopped

250 g (9 oz) firm tofu

4 tablespoons olive oil

185 g (7 oz/1½ cups) grated pumpkin (see Note)

100 g (4 oz/¾ cup) grated zucchini (courgette) (see Note)

1 onion, chopped

4 garlic cloves, crushed

4 small spring onions (scallions), finely chopped

2 tablespoons chopped coriander (cilantro) leaves

1 tablespoon Madras curry powder

150 g (6 oz/1 cup) wholemeal flour

50 g (2 oz/½ cup) grated parmesan cheese

oil, for deep-frying

**1  To make the dipping sauce**, place the yoghurt, garlic and mint in a bowl, season and mix together well. Add a little water, if needed.

**2  Blend the tofu** in a food processor or blender until finely processed.

**3  Heat the oil** in a frying pan. Add the pumpkin, zucchini, onion and garlic. Cook over medium heat, stirring occasionally, for 10 minutes, or until the vegetables are tender. Cool.

**4  Add the spring onion**, coriander, curry powder, 75 g (3 oz/½ cup) of wholemeal flour, all the parmesan, the tofu and 1 tablespoon salt and mix well. Roll a tablespoon of the mixture between your hands to form a ball, then repeat with remaining mixture. Coat the balls in the remaining flour.

**5  Fill a deep** heavy-based saucepan one-third full of oil and heat to 180°C (350°F), or until a cube of bread browns in 15 seconds. Cook the tofu and vegetable koftas in small batches for 2–3 minutes, or until golden brown. Drain on paper towels. Serve with the dipping sauce.

Note: When buying the vegetables, buy a piece of pumpkin that weighs about 400 g (14 oz) and 200 g (7 oz) zucchini.

# SPICY KOFTAS

**MAKES 45**

500 g (1 lb 2 oz) minced (ground) lamb

1 small onion, finely chopped

1 garlic clove, crushed

1 teaspoon ground coriander

1 teaspoon ground cumin

¼ teaspoon ground cinnamon

½ teaspoon finely chopped red chilli

1 teaspoon tomato paste (concentrated purée)

1 tablespoon chopped mint

1 tablespoon chopped coriander (cilantro) leaves

oil, for frying

**YOGHURT DIP**

1 tomato, peeled, seeded and chopped

½ Lebanese (short) cucumber, chopped

1 garlic clove, crushed

1 tablespoon chopped mint

125 g (4½ oz/½ cup) plain yoghurt

**1** **Combine the lamb,** onion, garlic, coriander, cumin, cinnamon, chilli, tomato paste and mint and coriander leaves in a large bowl and mix well using your hands. Season well, then roll into small balls (about 1½ teaspoons each).

**2** **Heat a little oil** in a large heavy-based frying pan over high heat. Cook the koftas in batches until well browned all over and cooked through. Drain on crumpled paper towels.

**3** **Combine the dip** ingredients in a small bowl; mix well.

**4** **Skewer each kofta** with a cocktail stick and serve with the dip. The dip can be made several hours ahead.

**Notes:** You can freeze the cooked koftas. When required, thaw, cover with foil and reheat in an ovenproof dish in a 180°C (350°F/Gas 4) oven for 5–10 minutes.

# CHICKEN SAN CHOY BAU

**MAKES ABOUT 36**

1½ tablespoons vegetable oil

¼ teaspoon sesame oil

3 garlic cloves, crushed

3 teaspoons grated fresh ginger

6 spring onions (scallions), thinly sliced

500 g (1 lb 2 oz) minced (ground) chicken

100 g (4 oz) drained water chestnuts, finely chopped

100 g (4 oz) drained bamboo shoots, finely chopped

60 ml (2 fl oz/¼ cup) oyster sauce

2 teaspoons soy sauce

60 ml (2 fl oz/¼ cup) sherry

1 teaspoon sugar

4 small witlof (chicory/Belgian endive) heads, bases trimmed

oyster sauce, to serve

**1**  **Heat the oils** in a wok or large frying pan, add the garlic, ginger and half the spring onion and stir-fry over high heat for 1 minute. Add mince. Continue cooking for about 4 minutes, or until just cooked, breaking up any lumps.

**2**  **Add the water** chestnuts, bamboo shoots, oyster and soy sauces, sherry, sugar and the remaining spring onion. Cook for 2–3 minutes, or until the liquid thickens a little.

**3**  **Allow the mixture** to cool slightly before dividing among the witlof leaves; you will need about 2 heaped teaspoons per leaf. Drizzle with oyster sauce and serve immediately.

**Note:** The filling can be made up to 2 days in advance and reheated just before assembling.

# CRUNCHY THAI CHICKEN AND PEANUT CAKES

**MAKES 24**

3 teaspoons grated palm sugar (jaggery) or soft brown sugar

1 tablespoon fish sauce

350 g (12 oz) minced (ground) chicken

120 g (4 oz/¾ cup) toasted peanuts, chopped

40 g (1½ oz/½ cup) fresh breadcrumbs

1 tablespoon red Thai curry paste

1 tablespoon lime juice

3 makrut (kaffir lime) leaves, very finely shredded

2 tablespoons sweet chilli sauce

2 tablespoons chopped coriander (cilantro)

125 ml (4 fl oz/½ cup) oil

1 banana leaf, cut into twenty-four 5 cm (2 inch) square pieces

sweet chilli sauce, extra, to serve

**1** **Dissolve the sugar** in the fish sauce, then place in a bowl with the minced chicken, peanuts, breadcrumbs, curry paste, lime juice, lime leaves, sweet chilli sauce and coriander. Mix well. Divide the mixture into 24 small balls; they will be quite soft. Flatten the balls into discs about 1.5 cm (½ inch) thick. Lay them in a single layer on a tray, cover with plastic wrap and refrigerate for 30 minutes.

**2** **Heat the oil** in a heavy-based frying pan and cook the cakes in batches for 2–3 minutes each side, or until firm and golden. Drain on crumpled paper towels.

**3** **Place a chicken** cake on each square of banana leaf and top with a dash of sweet chilli sauce. Secure with a toothpick for easier serving.

**Note:** The uncooked Thai chicken cakes will keep frozen for up to 2 months or refrigerated in a single layer for 1 day.

# LAMB KORMA ON MINI POPPADOMS

**MAKES 24**

350 g (12 oz) lamb backstrap or fillet,
 cut into 1.5 cm (½ inch) cubes

2 tablespoons korma curry paste

1 garlic clove, crushed

1 teaspoon ground coriander

125 g (5 oz/½ cup) thick plain yoghurt

oil, for deep-frying

24 round 4 cm (1½ inch) poppadoms
 (chilli flavour, if available)

1 tablespoon oil, extra

1½ tablespoons mango chutney

small coriander (cilantro) leaves,
 to garnish

**1    Combine the lamb,** curry paste, garlic, ground coriander
and half the yoghurt in a non-metallic bowl. Cover and
refrigerate for 1–2 hours.

**2    Meanwhile, fill a** deep heavy-based saucepan or deep-
fryer one-third full of oil and heat to 180°C (350°F), or until a
cube of bread browns in 15 seconds. Cook the poppadoms a
few at a time for a few seconds each, or until they are puffed
and lightly golden. Remove with a slotted spoon and drain on
crumpled paper towels.

**3    Heat a wok** over high heat, add the extra oil and swirl to
coat. Add the marinated lamb and cook in batches, stirring,
for 4–5 minutes, or until the lamb is cooked through. Spoon
a heaped teaspoon onto each poppadom and top with
½ teaspoon of the remaining yoghurt, then ¼ teaspoon of the
chutney. Garnish with a coriander leaf and serve immediately.

**Note:** Lamb korma can be cooked and frozen for up to
2 months, or refrigerated for 2–3 days. Reheat in a saucepan
over low heat until warm. To make chicken korma. use 350 g
(12 oz) diced chicken tenderloins.

# CURRY PUFFS

**MAKES 25**

1 tablespoon vegetable oil

4 spring onions (scallions), finely chopped

4 coriander (cilantro) roots, washed and finely chopped

1 garlic clove, finely chopped

1 teaspoon ground turmeric

1 teaspoon ground coriander

1 teaspoon curry powder

300 g (10½ oz) minced (ground) pork

1 tablespoon fish sauce

2 teaspoons shaved palm sugar (jaggery) or soft brown sugar

230 g (8 oz/1 cup) cooked mashed potato

65 g (2 oz/½ cup) frozen baby peas, thawed

5 sheets ready-rolled puff pastry

vegetable oil, for deep-frying

sweet chilli sauce or your choice of dipping sauce, to serve

**1 Heat the oil** in a wok and swirl to coat. Add the spring onion, coriander root and garlic and stir-fry over medium heat for 1 minute, or until softened but not browned. Stir in the turmeric, ground coriander and curry powder, then add the pork and stir-fry for 3–4 minutes, or until the meat changes colour. Add the fish sauce and palm sugar, and stir until the sugar has dissolved. Stir in the mashed potato and peas, mix well, then leave the mixture to cool.

**2 Cut five rounds** from each pastry sheet, using a 7.5 cm (3 inch) cutter. Put a tablespoon of filling in the centre of each round, then fold them over and pinch edges together to seal.

**3 Fill a wok** one-third full of oil and heat to 180°C (350°F), or until a cube of bread dropped in the oil browns in 15 seconds. Deep-fry curry puffs in batches until crisp and golden brown. Drain on crumpled paper towels. Serve warm with your choice of dipping sauce.

# DEEP-FRIED PORK DUMPLINGS WITH MUSTARD SAUCE

**SERVES 4–6**

300 g (11 oz) minced (ground) pork

4 spring onions (scallions), finely sliced

1 tablespoon yellow mustard seeds

2 tablespoons light soy sauce

8 water chestnuts, chopped

1 egg, well beaten

30 square or round gow gee (egg) dumpling wrappers

3 tablespoons English mustard

oil, for deep-frying

**1**  **Combine the minced pork**, spring onions, mustard seeds, soy, water chestnuts and beaten egg in a bowl. Mix well.

**2**  **Lay a gow gee** wrapper on a dry, flat surface and brush the edges with water. Spoon 2 teaspoons of the pork mixture in the middle of the wrapper. Fold over to enclose the filling in a triangular or semi-circlular shape. Pinch the edges together firmly to seal, making sure to expel as much air as possible. Use your fingers to make three or four small pleats in either side to gather the dough around the filling. Repeat with the remaining ingredients.

**3**  **To make the sauce**, put the mustard into a bowl and add 4 tablespoons of water gradually, stirring until smooth.

**4**  **Heat the oil** in a wok and deep-fry dumplings in batches for 1–2 minutes, or until golden brown and the filling is cooked through. Drain on crumpled paper towels Serve hot with the dipping sauce.

# PORK BALLS WRAPPED IN BETEL LEAVES

**SERVES 6–8**

375 g (13 oz) minced (ground) pork

1 heaped tablespoon red curry paste

1 egg, lightly beaten

2 spring onions (scallions), finely chopped

1 lemon grass stem, white part only, finely chopped

2 garlic cloves, crushed

5 cm (2 inch) piece ginger, finely chopped

1 large red chilli, seeded and finely chopped

3 tablespoons chopped coriander (cilantro) leaves

85 g (3 oz/⅔ cup) finely sliced green beans

1 teaspoon sesame oil

**DRESSING**

2 tablespoons sweet chilli sauce

2 tablespoons lime juice

2 tablespoons fish sauce

1 tablespoon grated palm sugar (jaggery) or soft brown sugar

**TO SERVE**

40 betel leaves

3 tablespoons fried shallots

1 handful coriander (cilantro) leaves

**1**  Line the base of a large steamer with baking paper and punch with holes.

**2**  Put the pork, curry paste, egg, spring onion, lemon grass, garlic, ginger, chilli, coriander, beans and 1 teaspoon of salt in a large bowl and mix until well combined. Roll mixture into walnut-sized balls then brush each ball lightly with sesame oil (alternatively, put a few drops of oil on your hands and roll them — replenish the oil every 3–4 balls). Place the balls in the prepared steamer and cover with a lid. Sit the steamer over a wok or saucepan of boiling water and steam for 10 minutes, or until cooked. Transfer to a serving bowl.

**3**  To make dressing, put the sweet chilli sauce, lime juice, fish sauce and sugar in a bowl and stir until well combined and the sugar has dissolved.

**4**  Put a stack of betel leaves on each serving plate so that your guests can make their own wraps. Place a pork ball on the matte side of the leaf, top with some fried shallots and coriander leaves and drizzle with the dressing.

# FALAFEL

## MAKES 30

150 g (6 oz/1 cup) dried split broad (fava) beans (see Note)

220 g (8 oz/1 cup) dried chickpeas

1 onion, roughly chopped

6 garlic cloves, roughly chopped

2 teaspoons ground coriander

1 tablespoon ground cumin

5 tablespoons chopped flat-leaf (Italian) parsley

¼ teaspoon chilli powder

½ teaspoon bicarbonate of soda (baking soda)

3 tablespoons chopped coriander (cilantro)

light oil, for deep-frying

**1** **Cover the broad** beans with 750 ml (26 fl oz/3 cups) water and leave to soak for 48 hours. (Drain the beans, rinse and cover with fresh water once or twice.) Place the chickpeas in a large bowl, cover with 750 ml (26 fl oz/3 cups) water and soak for 12 hours.

**2** **Drain the beans** and chickpeas and pat dry with paper towels. Process in a food processor with the onion and garlic until smooth.

**3** **Add the ground coriander**, cumin, parsley, chilli powder, bicarbonate of soda and coriander. Season with salt and pepper, and mix until well combined. Transfer to a large bowl, knead and leave for 30 minutes.

**4** **Shape tablespoons of** mixture into balls, flatten slightly, place on a tray and leave for 20 minutes.

**5** **Fill a deep,** heavy-based saucepan one-third full of oil and heat to 180°C (350°F), or until a cube of bread browns in 15 seconds. Cook the falafel in batches for 1–2 minutes, or until golden. Drain on paper towels. Serve with hummus, baba ghannouj and pitta bread.

**Note:** Split broad beans are available from specialist food stores.

# LENTIL PATTIES WITH CUMIN SKORDALIA

**MAKES 32**

185 g (7 oz/1 cup) brown lentils

1 teaspoon cumin seeds

90 g (3 oz/½ cup) burghul (bulgur wheat)

1 tablespoon olive oil

3 garlic cloves, crushed

4 spring onions (scallions), thinly sliced

1 teaspoon ground coriander

3 tablespoons chopped parsley

3 tablespoons chopped mint

2 eggs, lightly beaten

oil, for deep-frying

**SKORDALIA**

500 g (1 lb 2 oz) floury potatoes, cut into 2 cm (¾ inch) cubes

3 garlic cloves, crushed

½ teaspoon ground cumin

pinch of ground white pepper

185 ml (6 fl oz/¾ cup) olive oil

2 tablespoons white vinegar

**1**  **Place the lentils** in a saucepan, add 625 ml (21½ fl oz/ 2½ cups) water and bring to the boil. Reduce the heat to low and cook, covered, for 30 minutes, or until soft. Meanwhile, toast cumin in a dry frying pan over low heat for 1–2 minutes, or until fragrant. Grind.

**2**  **Remove the lentils** from the heat and stir in the burghul. Set aside to cool.

**3**  **Heat the oil** in a frying pan and cook the garlic and spring onion for 1 minute. Add the coriander and cumin and cook for 30 seconds. Add to the lentil mixture with the parsley, mint and egg. Mix well. Chill for 30 minutes.

**4**  **To make the skordalia**, cook the potato in a saucepan of boiling water for 10 minutes, or until very soft. Drain and mash until smooth. Add the garlic, cumin, white pepper and 1 teaspoon salt. Gradually add the oil, mixing with a wooden spoon. Add the vinegar.

**5**  **Roll tablespoons of** the lentil mixture into balls, then flatten slightly. Fill a deep heavy-based saucepan or deep-fryer one-third full of oil and heat to 180°C (350°F), or until a cube of bread browns in 15 seconds. Cook the patties in batches for 1–2 minutes, or until crisp and browned. Drain on paper towels. Serve with the skordalia.

# ARANCINI

**MAKES 10**

440 g (16 oz/2 cups) risotto rice

1 egg, lightly beaten

1 egg yolk

50 g (2 oz/½ cup) grated parmesan

plain (all-purpose) flour

2 eggs, lightly beaten

dry breadcrumbs, to coat

oil, for deep-frying

**MEAT SAUCE**

1 dried porcini mushroom

1 tablespoon olive oil

1 onion, chopped

125 g (5 oz) minced (ground) beef or veal

2 slices prosciutto, finely chopped

2 tablespoons tomato paste (concentrated purée)

80 ml (3 fl oz/⅓ cup) white wine

½ teaspoon dried thyme leaves

3 tablespoons finely chopped fresh parsley

**1** **Cook the rice** in boiling water for 20 minutes, or until just soft. Drain, without rinsing, and cool. Put in a large bowl and add the egg, egg yolk and parmesan. Stir until the rice sticks together. Cover and set aside.

**2** **To make the meat sauce,** soak the mushroom in hot water for 10 minutes to soften, then squeeze dry and chop finely. Heat the oil in a frying pan. Add the mushroom and onion and cook for 3 minutes, or until soft. Add the mince and cook, stirring, until browned. Add the prosciutto, tomato paste, wine, thyme and pepper to taste. Cook, stirring, for 5 minutes, or until all the liquid is absorbed. Stir in the parsley and set aside to cool.

**3** **With wet hands,** form the rice mixture into 10 balls. Wet your hands again and gently pull the balls apart. Place 3 teaspoons of the meat sauce in the centre of each. Reshape to enclose the filling. Roll in the flour, beaten egg and breadcrumbs and chill for 1 hour.

**4** **Fill a deep heavy-based** pan one-third full of oil and heat to 180°C (350°F), or until a cube of bread browns in 15 seconds. Deep-fry the croquettes, two at a time, for 3–4 minutes, or until golden brown. Drain on paper towels and keep warm while cooking the rest.

# POLENTA WEDGES WITH BOCCONCINI AND TOMATO

**MAKES 48**

| 1 tablespoon olive oil |
| 250 g (9 oz/1⅔ cups) polenta |
| 75 g (3 oz/¾ cup) grated parmesan cheese |
| 2½ tablespoons ready-made pesto |
| 150 g (6 oz) bocconcini, thinly sliced |
| 12 cherry tomatoes, cut into quarters |
| 4 tablespoons fresh basil, larger leaves torn |

**1** **Lightly grease a** 20 cm x 30 cm (8 x 12 inch) baking tin with the olive oil. Bring 1 litre (35 fl oz/4 cups) lightly salted water to the boil in a saucepan. Once the water is boiling, add the polenta in a steady stream, stirring continuously to prevent lumps forming. Reduce heat to very low and simmer, stirring regularly, for about 20–25 minutes, or until the polenta starts to come away from the side of the pan.

**2** **Stir the parmesan** into the polenta and season with salt and pepper. Spoon the polenta into the baking tray, smooth the top with the back of a wet spoon and leave for 1 hour, or until set.

**3** **Once the polenta** has set, carefully tip it out onto a board and cut into twenty-four 5 cm (2 inch) squares, then cut each square into two triangles. Chargrill the polenta in batches on a preheated chargrill pan for 2–3 minutes on each side, or until warmed through.

**4** **Spread each triangle** with 1 teaspoon of the pesto, top with a slice of bocconcini and a tomato quarter. Season and grill for 1–2 minutes, or until the cheese is just starting to melt. Garnish with basil and serve immediately.

# MINI LEEK PIES

**MAKES 32**

60 g (2 oz) butter

2 tablespoons olive oil

1 onion, finely chopped

3 leeks, finely sliced

1 garlic clove, chopped

1 tablespoon plain (all-purpose) flour

2 tablespoons sour cream

100 g (4 oz/1 cup) grated parmesan cheese

1 teaspoon chopped thyme

4 sheets frozen puff pastry, thawed

1 egg, lightly beaten

**1**  **Heat the butter** and oil in a large frying pan over medium heat. Add the onion and cook, stirring occasionally, for 2 minutes. Add the leek and garlic and cook for 5 minutes, or until the leek is softened and lightly coloured. Add the flour and stir into the mixture for 1 minute. Add the sour cream and stir until slightly thickened. Transfer to a bowl and add the parmesan and thyme. Season with salt and cracked black pepper and allow to cool.

**2**  **Preheat the oven** to 200°C (400°F/ Gas 6). Place a lightly greased baking tray in the oven to heat. Using a 6 cm (2½ inch) cutter, cut the pastry into 64 circles. Place 2 heaped teaspoons of filling on half the pastry circles, leaving a small border. Lightly brush the edges with egg, then place a pastry circle on top of each. Seal the edges well with a fork. Lightly brush the tops with egg.

**3**  **Place the pies** on the heated tray. Bake for 25 minutes, or until the pies are puffed and golden.

# MINI SPINACH PIES

MAKES 24

80 ml (3 fl oz/⅓ cup) olive oil

2 onions, finely chopped

2 garlic cloves, chopped

150 g (5½ oz) small button mushrooms, roughly chopped

200 g (7 oz) English spinach, chopped

½ teaspoon chopped thyme

100 g (3½ oz) feta cheese, crumbled

750 g (1 lb 10 oz) home-made or bought shortcrust pastry

milk, to glaze

**1** **Heat 2 tablespoons** of oil in a frying pan over medium heat and cook the onion and garlic for 5 minutes, or until soft and lightly coloured. Add the mushrooms and cook for 4 minutes, or until softened. Transfer to a bowl.

**2** **Heat 1 tablespoon** of oil in the same pan over medium heat, add half the spinach and cook, stirring well, for about 3 minutes, or until the spinach has softened. Add to the bowl with the onion. Repeat with the remaining oil and spinach. Add the thyme and feta to the bowl and mix. Season with salt and pepper and set aside to cool.

**3** **Preheat the oven** to 200°C (400°F/ Gas 6) and grease two 12-hole round-based mini muffin tins. Roll out half the pastry between two sheets of baking paper and cut out 24 rounds using a 7.5 cm (3 inch) cutter. Use these to line the muffin tins, then divide the spinach mixture among the holes. Roll out the remaining pastry between the baking paper sheets and cut out 24 rounds using a 7 cm (3 inch) cutter. Cover the pies with the lids and press the edges with a fork to seal. Prick the tops once with a fork, brush with milk and bake for 15–20 minutes, or until golden.

# BEEF AND VEGETABLE EMPANADAS

**MAKES 25**

1 tablespoon olive oil

1 small onion, finely chopped

2 garlic cloves, crushed

½ teaspoon freshly cracked black pepper

¼ teaspoon ground cinnamon

½ teaspoon ground allspice

250 g (9 oz) minced (ground) lean beef

250 g (9 oz/1 cup) tomato passata (puréed tomatoes)

1 small carrot, finely diced

1 small zucchini (courgette), finely diced

20 g (¾ oz) raisins

2 teaspoons cider vinegar

5 sheets frozen shortcrust pastry, thawed

1 egg, lightly beaten

vegetable oil, for deep-frying

sour cream, to serve

**1** **Heat the oil** in a heavy-based frying pan over medium–high heat. Cook onion, garlic and spices for 2 minutes, or until the onion is soft. Add the minced beef and cook for 5 minutes, or until brown. Stir in the tomato passata, vegetables, raisins and vinegar. Reduce heat and simmer, covered, for 15 minutes, then remove the lid and continue to simmer until thickened. Set aside and allow to cool.

**2** **Cut twenty-five 9 cm (3½ inch) rounds** from the pastry. Put 1 tablespoon of the beef and vegetable mixture in the centre of each round, and lightly brush the edges with the egg. Fold the pastry over to enclose the filling, press the edges and pinch to seal.

**3** **Fill a deep-fryer,** large saucepan or wok one-third full with vegetable oil and heat to 180°C (350°F), or until a cube of bread browns in 15 seconds. Fry the empanadas three at a time for 2–3 minutes, or until crisp and brown, then drain on paper towel. Serve with dollops of sour cream.

# HAM AND OLIVE EMPANADILLAS

**MAKES ABOUT 15**

2 hard-boiled eggs, roughly chopped

40 g (1½ oz) stuffed green olives, chopped

95 g (3¼ oz) ham, finely chopped

30 g (1 oz/¼ cup) grated cheddar cheese

3 sheets ready-rolled puff pastry

1 egg yolk, lightly beaten

**1** **Preheat the oven** to 220°C (425°F/Gas 7). Lightly grease two baking trays.

**2** **Combine the boiled eggs** with the olives, ham and cheese in a bowl. Cut the puff pastry sheets into 10 cm (4 inch) rounds (about five rounds from each sheet). Spoon a tablespoon of the ham and olive mixture into the centre of each round, fold over the pastry to enclose the filling and crimp the edges to seal.

**3** **Place the pastries** on the trays, spacing them 2 cm (¾ inch) apart. Brush with egg yolk; bake for 15 minutes, or until brown and puffed, swapping trays around in the oven after 10 minutes. Cover loosely with foil if pastry is browning too much. Serve hot.

# THAI CHICKEN SAUSAGE ROLLS

**MAKES 24**

200 g (7 oz) boneless, skinless chicken breasts, roughly chopped

150 g (6 oz) mild pancetta, chopped

1 garlic clove, crushed

3 spring onions (scallions), chopped

2 tablespoons chopped coriander (cilantro)

2 bird's eye chillies, seeded and finely chopped

1 teaspoon fish sauce

1 egg

1 teaspoon grated fresh ginger

375 g (13 oz) block frozen puff pastry

1 egg yolk

2 tablespoons sesame seeds

sweet chilli sauce, to serve

fresh coriander (cilantro), to serve

**1  Preheat the oven** to 180°C (350°F/Gas 4). Put the chicken, pancetta, garlic, spring onion, coriander, chilli, fish sauce, whole egg and ginger in a food processor and process until just combined.

**2  Roll out the pastry** to 30 x 40 cm (12 x 16 inches). Cut in half lengthways. Take half the filling and, using floured hands, roll it into a long sausage shape and place along the long edge of one piece of pastry. Brush the edges with a little water and fold over, pressing down to seal. Place the sealed edge underneath. Repeat with the remaining pastry and filling.

**3  Using a sharp knife**, cut the sausage rolls into 2.5 cm (1 inch) lengths on the diagonal; discard the end pieces. Brush the tops with egg yolk, then sprinkle with sesame seeds. Bake for 15 minutes, or until golden. Serve with sweet chilli sauce and garnished with coriander.

**Note:** You can make the sausage rolls a day before the party. Reheat in a (180°C/350°F/ Gas 4) oven for 10–12 minutes, or until warmed through.

# HONEY MUSTARD CHICKEN DRUMETTES

**MAKES 24**

80 ml (3 fl oz/⅓ cup) oil

90 g (3 oz/¼ cup) honey

60 ml (2 fl oz/¼ cup) soy sauce

60 g (2 oz/¼ cup) dijon mustard

60 ml (2 fl oz/¼ cup) lemon juice

40 garlic cloves, crushed

24 chicken drumettes (see Note)

**1   To make the marinade**, place the oil, honey, soy sauce, mustard, lemon juice and garlic in a large non-metallic dish and mix together thoroughly.

**2   Trim the chicken** of excess fat, place in the dish with the marinade and toss until well coated. Cover and refrigerate for at least 2 hours, or preferably overnight, turning 2–3 times.

**3   Preheat the oven** to 200°C (400°F/Gas 6). Place the drumettes on a wire rack over a foil-lined baking tray. Bake, turning and brushing with the marinade 3–4 times, for 45 minutes, or until golden brown and cooked. Serve immediately with serviettes for sticky fingers.

**Notes:** Drumettes are the chicken wing with the wing tip removed. Cook a day ahead; reheat in a 160°C (315°F/Gas 2-3) oven for 10-12 minutes.

# LEMON GRASS PRAWNS

**MAKES 24**

6 lemon grass stalks, cut in half lengthways, then in half crossways

1 kg (2 lb 4 oz) peeled and deveined prawns (shrimp)

3 spring onions (scallions), roughly chopped

4 tablespoons coriander (cilantro) leaves

2 tablespoons fresh mint

2 tablespoons fish sauce

1½ tablespoons lime juice

1–2 tablespoons sweet chilli sauce, plus extra for serving

peanut oil, for brushing

**1**  **Soak the lemon grass** in water for 30 minutes, then pat dry. Process the prawns, spring onion, coriander, mint, fish sauce, lime juice and chilli sauce in a food processor. Take a tablespoon of the mix and mould around the end of a lemon grass stalk, using wet hands. Refrigerate for 30 minutes.

**2**  **Brush a barbecue hotplate** or chargrill pan with the oil. Cook the skewers, turning occasionally, for 5 minutes, or until cooked. Serve with sweet chilli sauce.

# SATAY CHICKEN STICKS

### MAKES 24

8 large chicken tenderloins, trimmed
    and sliced into thirds lengthways

1 garlic clove, crushed

3 teaspoons fish sauce

2 teaspoons grated fresh ginger

24 fresh makrut (kaffir lime) leaves

lime wedges, to serve

### SATAY SAUCE

2 teaspoons peanut oil

4 red Asian shallots, finely chopped

2 garlic cloves, chopped

2 teaspoons grated fresh ginger

2 small red chillies, finely chopped

200 ml (7 fl oz) coconut milk

125 g (4½ fl oz/½ cup) crunchy peanut
    butter

2 tablespoons grated palm sugar
    (jaggery) or soft brown sugar

2 tablespoons lime juice

1½ tablespoons fish sauce

2 teaspoons soy sauce

1 makrut (kaffir lime) leaf

**1** **Combine the chicken,** garlic, fish sauce and ginger. Cover, then refrigerate for 1 hour.

**2** **To make the sauce**, heat the oil in a saucepan over medium heat. Add the shallots, garlic, ginger and chilli and cook for 5 minutes, or until golden. Add the rest of the ingredients, reduce the heat and simmer for 10 minutes, or until thick.

**3** **Thread a lime leaf** and a chicken strip onto each skewer, then cook on a hot barbecue hotplate or chargrill pan for 3–4 minutes. Serve with satay sauce and lime wedges.

# THAI FISH CAKES

## MAKES 24

### CHILLI LIME DIPPING SAUCE

1 small red chilli, seeded and finely chopped

1 teaspoon caster (superfine) sugar

1½ tablespoons rice vinegar

1½ tablespoons lime juice

2 tablespoons fish sauce

¼ small carrot, finely chopped

¼ small Lebanese (short) cucumber, seeded and finely chopped

600 g (1 lb 5 oz) skinless firm white fish fillets (such as ling, bream or redfish)

2 tablespoons Thai red curry paste

2 tablespoons fish sauce

3 teaspoons lime juice

1 egg, lightly beaten

2 tablespoons finely chopped coriander (cilantro) leaves and roots

4 makrut (kaffir lime) leaves, finely chopped

150 g (5½ oz) snake (yard-long) beans, finely chopped

24 mint leaves

1    **To make the dipping sauce,** combine all the ingredients and 3 tablespoons of water in a bowl and stir until the sugar has dissolved and the ingredients are well combined.

2    **Put the fish,** curry paste, fish sauce and lime juice in a food processor and blend until a smooth, sticky paste is formed. Transfer to a large non-metallic bowl and add egg, coriander, lime leaves, snake beans and ½ teaspoon of salt. Using your hands, mix until ingredients are well combined.

3    **Line a large steamer** with baking paper and punch with holes. Shape tablespoons of the fish mixture into 24 small balls, then flatten gently with the palm of your hand to form patties. Arrange patties in the steamer, making sure they don't touch each other (use a second steamer, if necessary). Put a mint leaf on top of each patty; cover steamer with a lid. Sit the steamer over a wok or a pan of simmering water and steam for about 10 minutes, or until cooked through. Remove from heat and serve immediately with the chilli lime dipping sauce.

# SUGAR CANE PRAWNS

**MAKES 10**

500 g (1 lb 2 oz) raw prawns (shrimp), peeled, deveined and roughly chopped

2 tablespoons chopped coriander (cilantro) leaves

2 tablespoons chopped mint

1 lemon grass stem, white part only, finely chopped

1 small red chilli, seeded and finely chopped

1 garlic clove, crushed

1½ tablespoons fish sauce

2 teaspoons lime juice

½ teaspoon sugar

10 pieces of sugar cane, about 10 cm (4 inches) long and 5 mm (¼ inch) wide (see Note)

lime wedges, to serve

**1**  **Put the prawns,** coriander, mint, lemon grass, chilli, garlic, fish sauce, lime juice, sugar and ¼ teaspoon of salt in a food processor and blend until smooth.

**2**  **With wet hands,** roll 2 tablespoons of mixture into a ball, then mould around the middle of a sugar cane skewer, pressing firmly to secure. Repeat with remaining mixture and sugar cane, then refrigerate for 15 minutes.

**3**  **Line a steamer** with baking paper and punch with holes. Arrange the skewers on top in a single layer and cover with a lid. Sit the steamer over a wok or saucepan of boiling water and steam for 7–8 minutes, or until cooked through.

**4**  **Serve the skewers** with lime wedges or with a quick dipping sauce made up of sweet chilli sauce mixed with a little fish sauce.

**Note:** If you can't find fresh sugar cane, the tinned version can be used. Look for it in Asian food stores.

# PRAWN NORI ROLLS

## MAKES 25 ROLLS

500 g (1 lb 2 oz) raw prawns (shrimp), peeled and deveined

1½ tablespoons fish sauce

1 tablespoon sake

2 tablespoons chopped coriander (cilantro) leaves

1 large makrut (kaffir lime) leaf, finely shredded

1 tablespoon lime juice

2 teaspoons sweet chilli sauce

1 egg white, lightly beaten

5 sheets of nori

### DIPPING SAUCE

3 tablespoons sake

3 tablespoons light soy sauce

1 tablespoon mirin

1 tablespoon lime juice

**1** Put the prawns, fish sauce, sake, coriander, lime leaf, lime juice and sweet chilli sauce in a food processor and blend until smooth. Add the egg white and pulse for a few seconds to just combine.

**2** Lay the nori sheets on a flat surface, shiny-side-down, and spread some prawn mixture over each sheet, leaving a 2 cm (¾ inch) border at one end. Roll up tightly, cover and refrigerate for 1 hour to firm. Using a sharp knife, trim the ends and cut into 2 cm (¾ inch) lengths.

**3** Line a steamer with baking paper and punch with holes. Arrange the rolls in the steamer in a single layer and cover with a lid. Sit the steamer over a wok or saucepan of boiling water and steam for 5 minutes, or until cooked.

**4** To make the dipping sauce, mix together all the ingredients in a small bowl. Serve with the nori rolls.

# PORK AND PRAWN DUMPLINGS

### MAKES 24

300 g (10½ oz) minced (ground) pork

300 g (10½ oz) minced (ground) prawns (shrimp)

3 spring onions (scallions), finely sliced

60 g (2¼ oz/⅓ cup) chopped water chestnuts

1½ teaspoons finely chopped fresh ginger

1 tablespoon light soy sauce, plus extra, to serve

1 teaspoon caster (superfine) sugar

24 won ton wrappers

chilli sauce, to serve

**1**  **To make the filling**, put the pork and prawn meat, spring onion, water chestnuts, ginger, soy sauce and sugar in a large non-metallic bowl and combine well.

**2**  **Working with one wrapper** at a time, place a heaped tablespoon of filling in the centre of the wrapper. Bring the sides up around the outside, forming pleats to firmly encase the filling — the top of the dumpling should be exposed. Pinch together to enclose the bottom of the filling, then cover with a damp cloth. Repeat with the remaining wrappers and filling to make 24 in total.

**3**  **Line a large steamer** with baking paper and punch with holes. Place dumplings on top in a single layer, making sure they don't touch one another. Cover with a lid. Sit the steamer over a wok or saucepan of boiling water and steam for about 10 minutes, or until cooked through. Serve the dumplings with the soy and chilli sauces, for dipping.

**Note:** If you prefer, these dumplings can be made without the prawns — just double the amount of pork.

# DEEP-FRIED PORK AND PRAWN WON TONS

## MAKES 24

### FILLING

120 g (4½ oz) minced (ground) pork

3 raw king prawns (shrimp), peeled and deveined, finely sliced

4 water chestnuts, finely chopped

1 tablespoon oyster sauce

1 teaspoon soy sauce

½ teaspoon sesame oil

1 French or red Asian shallot, finely sliced

2 teaspoons cornflour (cornstarch)

24 won ton wrappers

vegetable oil, for deep-frying

sweet chilli sauce, to serve

**1** **To make the filling,** combine all the ingredients in a bowl and mix well. Cover and refrigerate until ready to use. If you can, make the filling a day in advance to give the flavours time to develop.

**2** **Put a heaped teaspoon** of filling in the centre of each won ton wrapper and lightly brush the edges with water. Fold the wrapper over to enclose filling and form a triangle.

**3** **Fill a wok** one-third full of oil and heat to 190°C (375°F), or until a cube of bread dropped in the oil browns in 10 seconds. Add won tons in batches and cook for 1–2 minutes, or until they are golden and crisp and the filling is cooked. Drain on crumpled paper towels and serve hot with sweet chilli sauce for dipping.

# VEGETABLE DUMPLINGS

## MAKES 25

1 tablespoon oil

3 spring onions (scallions), sliced

2 garlic cloves, chopped

2 teaspoons grated fresh ginger

3 tablespoons snipped garlic chives

425 g (15 oz/1 bunch) choy sum, shredded

2 tablespoons sweet chilli sauce

3 tablespoons chopped coriander (cilantro) leaves

40 g (1½ oz/¼ cup) tinned water chestnuts, drained and chopped

25 round gow gee dumpling wrappers

### DIPPING SAUCE

½ teaspoon sesame oil

½ teaspoon peanut oil

1 tablespoon soy sauce

1 tablespoon lime juice

1 small red chilli, seeded and finely chopped

**1** **Heat the oil** in a frying pan over medium heat and cook the spring onion, garlic, ginger and chives for 1–2 minutes, or until soft. Increase the heat to high, add the choy sum and cook for 4–5 minutes, or until wilted. Stir in the chilli sauce, coriander and water chestnuts. Allow to cool. If the mixture is too wet, squeeze dry.

**2** **Lay a wrapper** on the work surface. Place a heaped teaspoon of the filling in the centre. Moisten the edge of the wrapper with water and pinch to seal, forming a ball. Repeat with remaining wrappers and filling to make 25 dumplings.

**3** **Line a steamer** with baking paper and punch with holes. Arrange the dumplings, seam-side-up, in the steamer in a single layer and cover with a lid. Sit the steamer over a wok or saucepan of boiling water and steam for 5–6 minutes, or until the dumpling wrappers have softened and the filling is cooked.

**4** **Meanwhile, to make** the dipping sauce, combine all the ingredients in a small bowl. Serve with the dumplings.

# PORK AND PRAWN GOW GEES

**MAKES 30**

200 g (7 oz) raw prawn (shrimp) meat

200 g (7 oz) minced (ground) pork

5 spring onions (scallions), chopped

2 garlic cloves, crushed

1½ teaspoons grated fresh ginger

1 teaspoon sesame oil

1½ tablespoons soy sauce

1 tablespoon Chinese rice wine

30 gow gee wrappers

oil, for deep-frying

**DIPPING SAUCE**

3 tablespoons soy sauce

1 tablespoon Chinese rice wine

2.5 cm (1 inch) piece fresh ginger, cut into very thin strips

**1**  To make the dipping sauce, combine all the ingredients in a small bowl.

**2**  Put the prawn meat, pork, spring onion, garlic, ginger, sesame oil, soy sauce and rice wine in a food processor and blend until combined.

**3**  Put a heaped teaspoon of the mixture in the centre of each gow gee wrapper. Lightly brush the edges with a little water and fold over to form a half-moon shape. Press the edges together and fold to form small pleats.

**4**  Fill a wok one-third full of oil and heat it to 180°C (350°F), or until a cube of bread dropped into it browns in 15 seconds. Add gow gees in four batches and deep-fry for 2–3 minutes, or until golden and cooked through. Drain on crumpled paper towels. Serve hot with the dipping sauce.

# MUSHROOM AND WATER CHESTNUT STEAMED BUNS

**MAKES 24**

**DOUGH**

600 g (1 lb 5 oz/4¾ cups) plain (all-purpose) flour

2 tablespoons baking powder

2 tablespoons caster (superfine) sugar

3 tablespoons peanut oil

2 tablespoons oil

2 garlic cloves, finely chopped

1 teaspoon finely grated fresh ginger

1 small red chilli, seeded and finely sliced

8 Swiss brown mushrooms, finely chopped

8 shiitake mushrooms, finely chopped

225 g (8 oz) tin water chestnuts, drained and finely chopped

2 tablespoons oyster sauce

1 tablespoon soy sauce

1 teaspoon cornflour (cornstarch) mixed with 1 tablespoon water

2 spring onions (scallions), chopped

1 tablespoon chopped coriander (cilantro) leaves

**1** **To make the** dough, sift the flour, baking powder, sugar and 1 teaspoon of salt into a bowl. Gradually stir in the oil and 375 ml (13 fl oz/1½ cups) of water and mix to a soft dough. Turn dough out onto a floured board and knead for 5 minutes, or until the dough is smooth and elastic. Cover and let the dough rest at room temperature for 1 hour.

**2** **Meanwhile, heat the** oil in a frying pan over medium heat, add the garlic, ginger and chilli and cook for 1 minute, or until softened. Stir in all the mushrooms and cook for a further 5 minutes, or until the mushrooms are tender. Add the water chestnuts, oyster sauce, soy sauce and combined cornflour and water and simmer, stirring, for about 1 minute, or until the mixture has thickened slightly. Remove from the heat and stir in the spring onion and coriander. Set aside to cool.

**3** **Divide the dough** into 24 pieces. Shape each piece into a 6 cm (2½ inch) flat round. Put 1 teaspoon of mushroom mixture in the centre of each and gather the edges together, pinching to enclose the filling.

**4** **Line a steamer** with baking paper and punch with holes. Place the buns on top, 2 cm (¾ inch) apart, and cover with a lid (you may need to do this in batches).

**5** **Sit the steamer** over a wok or saucepan of boiling water and steam for about 15–20 minutes, or until the buns are firm. Serve immediately.

# OYSTER PO' BOYS

**MAKES 18**

60 g (2 oz/½ cup) self-raising flour

¼ teaspoon cayenne pepper

¼ teaspoon paprika

1 small egg

125 ml (4 fl oz/½ cup) milk

vegetable oil, for deep-frying

18 oysters, shucked

**1 Sift the flour,** cayenne pepper, paprika and a pinch of salt into a bowl.

**2 Beat the egg** and milk together and gradually add to the flour, whisking to give a smooth batter.

**3 Fill a deep-fat fryer** or large saucepan one-third full of oil. Heat to 180°C (350°F), or until a cube of bread dropped into the oil turns golden brown in 15 seconds. Pat dry the oysters, dip into the batter and deep-fry in batches for 1–2 minutes, or until golden brown. Drain on crumpled paper towels and serve at once as they are or sandwiched between crusty bread.

# DEEP-FRIED PRAWNS WITH DIPPING SAUCE

## MAKES 24

55 g (2 oz/½ cup) besan (chickpea) flour

60 g (2 oz/½ cup) self-raising flour

1 teaspoon grated fresh ginger

1 garlic clove, crushed

½ teaspoon ground turmeric

### LEMON AND GINGER DIPPING SAUCE

4 tablespoons lemon juice

2 tablespoons grated palm sugar (jaggery) or soft brown sugar

1 tablespoon fish sauce

2 teaspoons grated fresh ginger

1 garlic clove, crushed

24 raw prawns (shrimp), peeled and deveined, tails intact

vegetable oil, for deep-frying

**1** **Sift the besan** and self-raising flours into a bowl and make a well in the centre. Combine the ginger, garlic and turmeric with 250 ml (9 fl oz/1 cup) of water and add to the sifted flours all at once. Using a whisk, combine the ingredients to form a smooth batter. Set aside.

**2** **To make the dipping sauce**, combine the ingredients in a bowl, stirring to dissolve the palm sugar.

**3** **Pat the prawns** dry with paper towels and slit along the belly to butterfly them, being careful not to cut all the way through. Fill a wok one-third full of oil and heat to 170°C (325°F), or until a cube of bread dropped in the oil browns in 20 seconds. Holding onto the tails, dip the prawns in the batter, leaving the tails undipped. Deep-fry a few at a time until golden; drain on crumpled paper towels. Serve warm with the dipping sauce.

# STUFFED SHIITAKE

SERVES 4–6

STUFFING

300 g (11 oz) raw prawns (shrimp), peeled, deveined and finely chopped

150 g (5½ oz) minced (ground) chicken

50 g (1¾ oz) pork rind, very finely chopped (ask your butcher for this)

30 g (1 oz) ham, finely chopped

1 spring onion (scallion), finely chopped

2 large garlic cloves, crushed

1½ tablespoons finely chopped water chestnuts

1½ tablespoons finely chopped bamboo shoots

1½ teaspoons grated fresh ginger

1 tablespoon Chinese rice wine

1 tablespoon oyster sauce

1 tablespoon light soy sauce

2–3 drops of sesame oil

1 egg white, beaten until frothy

¼ teaspoon sugar

pinch of Chinese five-spice

white pepper, to taste

300 g (11 oz) shiitake mushrooms (see Note)

1 litre (35 fl oz/4 cups) chicken stock

1 star anise

oyster sauce, to serve

toasted sesame seeds, to garnish (optional)

**1  To make the stuffing**, put the prawns, chicken, pork rind, ham, spring onion, garlic, water chestnuts, bamboo shoots, ginger, rice wine, oyster sauce, soy sauce, sesame oil, egg white, sugar, five-spice and white pepper in a bowl and mix together thoroughly.

**2  Remove the stalks** from shiitake and reserve. Generously fill each mushroom cap with the stuffing, rounding the tops slightly. The amount of stuffing you use for each mushroom will differ depending on their size.

**3  Pour the chicken stock** and 500 ml (17 fl oz/2 cups) of water into a wok. Add the star anise and reserved mushroom stalks. Bring to the boil over high heat, then reduce the heat and keep at a slow boil.

**4  Line a large steamer** with baking paper and punch with holes. Place the mushrooms in a single layer on top, filling side up. Cover with a lid, sit the steamer over the boiling stock mixture and steam for 15 minutes, or until the filling and the mushrooms are cooked through. Place on a serving platter and pour on a little of the stock. Drizzle with a little oyster sauce and garnish with the sesame seeds.

**Note:** When purchasing fresh shiitake, choose mushrooms that are plump, with firm caps that curl under. Avoid any with shrivelled, dehydrated caps as they are well past their peak. Choose mushrooms of a similar size so they cook evenly.

# PORK AND NOODLE BALLS WITH SWEET CHILLI SAUCE

MAKES 30

DIPPING SAUCE

80 ml (3 fl oz/⅓ cup) sweet chilli sauce

2 teaspoons mirin

2 teaspoons finely chopped fresh ginger

125 ml (4 fl oz/½ cup) Japanese soy sauce

250 g (9 oz) hokkien noodles

300 g (11 oz) minced (ground) pork

6 spring onions (scallions), finely chopped

2 garlic cloves, crushed

6 tablespoons finely chopped coriander (cilantro) leaves

1 tablespoon fish sauce

2 tablespoons oyster sauce

1½ tablespoons lime juice

peanut oil, for deep-frying

**1**　**To make the dipping sauce**, combine the sweet chilli sauce, mirin, ginger and Japanese soy sauce in a bowl.

**2**　**Place the noodles** in a bowl and cover with boiling water. Soak for 1 minute, or until tender. Drain very well and pat dry with paper towels. Cut the noodles into 5 cm (2 inch) lengths, then transfer to a large bowl. Add the minced pork, spring onion, garlic, coriander leaves, fish sauce, oyster sauce and lime juice and combine the mixture well using your hands, making sure the pork is evenly distributed throughout the noodles.

**3**　**Roll 1 tablespoon** of mixture at a time into a ball, making 30 in total. Press each ball firmly to ensure it holds its shape during cooking.

**4**　**Fill a wok** or large saucepan one-third full of oil. Heat to 170°C (325°F), or until a cube of bread browns in 20 seconds. Deep-fry pork balls in batches for 2–3 minutes, or until golden and cooked through. Drain on paper towels. Serve hot with the dipping sauce.

Note: The dipping sauce is best made up to a week ahead to allow the flavours to develop.

# PRAWN, CORN AND CORIANDER FRITTERS

MAKES 18

500 g (1 lb 2 oz) small peeled raw prawns (shrimp), finely chopped

4 spring onions (scallions), chopped

2 garlic cloves, crushed

3 tablespoons chopped coriander (cilantro) leaves

1½ tablespoons fish sauce

1 egg, lightly beaten

30 g (1 oz/¼ cup) potato flour or cornflour

2 x 125 g (5 oz) tins corn kernels, drained

oil, for deep-frying

sweet chilli sauce, to serve

1  **Put the prawns,** spring onion, garlic, coriander, fish sauce, egg and flour in a food processor and process until well combined. Fold in the corn. Using 2 tablespoons of mixture at a time, form into 18 rounds (the mixture may be very sticky). Transfer to a bowl, cover and refrigerate for 30 minutes.

2  **Fill a wok** one-third full of oil and heat to 180°C (350°F), or until a cube of bread dropped in the oil browns in 15 seconds. Deep-fry the cakes for 2 minutes, or until they are golden and cooked through. Drain on crumpled paper towels and serve with sweet chilli sauce or a dipping sauce of your choice.

# TEMPURA WITH SOY AND GINGER DIPPING SAUCE

SERVES 4

200 g (7 oz) shelled large prawns (shrimp), peeled and deveined, tails intact

300 g (11 oz) skinned haddock fillets

2 teaspoons finely grated fresh ginger

1 tablespoon mirin

100 ml (4 fl oz) soy sauce

vegetable oil, for deep-frying

250 g (9 oz/2 cups) tempura flour (see Note)

1 large egg, lightly beaten

270 ml (9½ fl oz/1 cup and 1 tablespoon) iced water

### FISH SUBSTITUTION

bream, cod, rock cod, squid, lobster, crayfish

**1**  **Make three cuts** on the underside of each prawn and straighten them out. Cut the fish into bite-sized chunks.

**2**  **Mix the ginger** and mirin into the soy sauce, and dilute to taste with up to 2½ tablespoons of water. Pour the sauce into dipping bowls.

**3**  **Fill a deep-fat** fryer or large saucepan one-third full of oil and heat to 180°C (350°F), or until a cube of white bread dropped into the oil turns golden brown in 15 seconds.

**4**  **Put the flour** into a large bowl. Whisk the egg into the iced water. Very lightly whisk the iced water and egg into the tempura flour—it should still be lumpy. If you overwork the batter at this stage, you will not end up with a light coating. Dip the prawns and fish in the batter in batches and fry until crisp and golden. Drain on crumpled paper towels and serve immediately with the dipping sauce.

Note: Tempura flour is an especially fine flour available at Asian supermarkets. If you can't find it, use 185 g (1½ cups) plain (all-purpose) flour mixed with 90 g (½ cup) rice flour.

# BOREK

**MAKES 24**

400 g (14 oz) feta cheese

2 eggs, lightly beaten

5 tablespoons chopped flat-leaf (Italian)
parsley

375 g (13 oz) filo pastry

80 ml (3 fl oz/⅓ cup) olive oil

**1** **Preheat the oven** to 180°C (350°F/ Gas 4). Lightly grease a baking tray. Crumble the feta into a large bowl using a fork or your fingers. Mix in the eggs and parsley and season with freshly ground black pepper.

**2** **Cover the filo pastry** with a damp tea towel so it doesn't dry out. Remove one sheet at a time. Brushing each sheet lightly with olive oil, layer four sheets on top of one another. Cut the pastry into four 7 cm (2¾ inch) strips.

**3** **Place two rounded teaspoons** of the feta mixture in one corner of each strip and fold diagonally, creating a triangle pillow. Place on the baking tray, seam-side-down, and brush with olive oil. Repeat with the remaining pastry and filling to make 24 parcels. Bake for 20 minutes, or until golden. Serve these as part of a meze plate.

**Note:** Fillings for borek are versatile and can be adapted to include your favourite cheeses such as haloumi, gruyère, cheddar or mozzarella.

# PETIT CROQUE-MONSIEUR

### MAKES 24

1 loaf of bread, sliced into 6 slices lengthways

125 g (5 oz/½ cup) wholegrain mustard

100 g (4 oz) thinly shaved honey ham

100 g (4 oz) thinly sliced jarlsberg cheese

55 g (2 oz/⅓ cup) very finely chopped mustard fruits (optional) (see Note)

40 g (1½ oz) butter

2 tablespoons olive oil

**1** **Brush each slice** of bread with 1 tablespoon of mustard. Divide the ham and cheese into three portions and lay one portion of the ham, then the cheese, on three bread slices. If you are using mustard fruits, sprinkle them over the cheese. Press the other bread slices, mustard-side-down, on top so that you have three large sandwiches.

**2** **Cut eight rounds** from each sandwich, using a 5 cm (2 inch) cutter. Melt half the butter and oil in a non-stick frying pan and, when the butter begins to foam, cook half the rounds until crisp and golden and the cheese is just starting to melt. Keep warm on a baking tray in a warm oven while you cook the remaining rounds. Serve warm.

**Note:** Mustard fruits are also known as mostarda di frutta and are available in jars at specialty supermarkets and delis.

# MINI STEAK SANDWICHES

**MAKES 20**

100 ml (4 fl oz) olive oil

1 onion, thinly sliced

1 large handful parsley

10 large basil leaves

20 mint leaves

1 garlic clove, crushed

1 tablespoon dijon mustard

1 tablespoon capers

2 anchovy fillets

400 g (14 oz) fillet steak, about 1 cm (½ inch) thick

1 baguette, cut into 40 x 5 mm (¼ inch) slices

**1**  **Heat 2 tablespoons** of oil in a frying pan and cook the onion over low heat for 25 minutes, or until caramelized.

**2**  **To make the salsa verde**, place the parsley, basil, mint, garlic, mustard, capers, anchovies and the remaining oil in a food processor and pulse to a thick paste. Season.

**3**  **Cut out 20 rounds** from the steak with a 2.5 cm (1 inch) cutter. Season, then sear on a lightly oiled chargrill pan on both sides for 1–2 minutes, or until cooked to your liking. Put a little of the onion on 20 rounds of bread, top with a piece of steak and a dollop of salsa verde, then top with the remaining bread. Serve warm.

# MINI FOCACCIA WITH ROASTED VEGETABLES

### MAKES 24

2 red capsicums (peppers)

2 yellow capsicums (peppers)

3 slender eggplants (aubergines)

2 large zucchini (courgettes)

1 red onion

80 ml (3 fl oz/⅓ cup) extra virgin olive oil

3 garlic cloves, crushed

12 mini focaccias, halved

60 g (2 oz/¼ cup) ready-made pesto

3 large bocconcini (fresh baby mozarella cheese), sliced

**1** **Preheat the oven** to 200°C (400°F/Gas 6). Cut the red and yellow capsicums into 2.5 cm (1 inch) pieces. Slice the eggplants and zucchini into 1 cm (½ inch) rounds, then thinly slice the onion. Place all the vegetables in a roasting tin with the oil and garlic. Season with salt and cracked black pepper and toss together well. Roast for 25 minutes, or until cooked.

**2** **Spread each half** of the focaccia with ½ teaspoon of the pesto and divide the vegetables among them. Place two slices of bocconcini on top of each base, then top with the lid. Toast the focaccias on both sides on a hot chargrill pan until heated through.

**3** **Slice each focaccia** in half, then wrap a 2.5 cm (1 inch) wide band of double baking paper around the middle of the sandwiches and secure with string. Serve warm.

# MINI SPICY PORK QUESADILLAS

**MAKES 24**

2¾ tablespoons olive oil

½ teaspoon ground oregano

1 teaspoon ground cumin

½ teaspoon garlic salt

½ teaspoon cayenne pepper

350 g (12 oz) minced (ground) pork

2–3 chopped jalapeño chillies in brine

30 g (1 oz/¼ cup) pitted black olives, sliced

55 g (2 oz/⅓ cup) green olives stuffed with red pimentos, sliced

2 tablespoons chopped coriander (cilantro) leaves

12 x 16 cm (6¼ in) flour tortillas

60 g (2 oz/½ cup) grated mild cheddar cheese

75 g (3 oz/½ cup) grated mozzarella cheese

coriander (cilantro) sprigs, to garnish

**1   To make the spicy pork** mince, heat 1½ tablespoons of the olive oil in a large frying pan; when hot add the oregano, cumin, garlic salt and cayenne pepper and cook for 30 seconds. Add the minced pork and cook over high heat for 10 minutes, before incorporating the chillies and all the olives. Cook for another 5 minutes, then stir in the chopped coriander. Remove from the heat and allow to cool.

**2   Cut each tortilla** in half. Place 1 tablespoon of filling on one half of each half. Mix the cheeses together, then put 1 tablespoon of the grated cheese on top of the spicy pork mince. Turn the flap of tortilla over the filling and press down firmly.

**3   Heat 2 teaspoons** of the remaining oil in a non-stick frying pan over high heat and cook the quesadillas in batches of six for 3–4 minutes each side, or until golden. Add a teaspoon of oil to the pan after each batch. Garnish with coriander sprigs.

**Note:** For a very simple vegetarian filling, simply sprinkle each half tortilla with 1 tablespoon chopped tomato, chilli, olives and coriander, then the cheese; fold over and cook as for the pork quesadillas.

# TURKISH PIZZA

MAKES 24

**BASIC PIZZA DOUGH**

10 g (½ oz) dried yeast

1 teaspoon caster (superfine) sugar

500 g (1 lb 2 oz/4 cups) plain (all-purpose) flour

2 tablespoons olive oil

1 tablespoon olive oil, plus extra for brushing

375 g (13 oz) minced (ground) lamb

1 onion, finely chopped

40 g (1½ oz/¼ cup) pine nuts

1 tomato, peeled, seeded and chopped

¼ teaspoon ground cinnamon

pinch of allspice

2 teaspoons chopped coriander (cilantro), plus extra for serving

2 teaspoons lemon juice

60 g (2 oz/¼ cup) plain yoghurt

**1  Combine the yeast,** sugar and 185 ml (6 fl oz/¾ cup) warm water. Cover and leave for 10 minutes, or until frothy. If it hasn't foamed after 10 minutes, discard and start again.

**2  Sift the flour** with ½ teaspoon salt and make a well in the centre. Add the yeast mixture and oil. Mix with a flat-bladed knife, using a cutting action, until a dough forms. Knead for 10 minutes, or until smooth. Place in an oiled bowl, cover with plastic wrap and leave for 45 minutes, or until doubled in size.

**3  Heat the oil** in a frying pan over medium heat and cook the mince for 3 minutes, or until browned. Add the onion and cook over low heat for 8 minutes, or until soft. Add the pine nuts, tomato, spices, ¼ teaspoon cracked pepper and some salt. Cook for 8 minutes, or until dry. Stir in the coriander and lemon juice and season.

**4  Preheat the oven** to 230°C (450°F/Gas 8). Punch down dough, then knead for 8 minutes, or until elastic. Roll out into 24 ovals. Spoon some filling onto each base. Pinch together the two short sides to form a boat shape. Brush with oil, and place the pizzas on a greased baking tray. Bake for 10 minutes. Serve with a dab of yoghurt and some coriander.

# PRAWN AND PESTO PIZZA

MAKES 24

PIZZA DOUGH

7 g (½ oz) sachet dried yeast

½ teaspoon caster (superfine) sugar

250 g (9 oz/2 cups) plain (all-purpose) flour

1 tablespoon olive oil

2 tablespoons olive oil

1 teaspoon finely chopped fresh basil

1 garlic clove, crushed

24 cooked medium prawns (shrimp), peeled and deveined

60 g (2 oz/¼ cup) ready-made pesto

24 small fresh basil leaves

24 pine nuts

1   **Combine the yeast,** sugar and 185 ml (6 fl oz/¾ cup) warm water, cover and leave for 10 minutes, or until frothy. If it hasn't foamed after 10 minutes, discard and start again.

2   **Sift the flour** and ½ teaspoon salt and make a well. Add the yeast mixture and the oil. Mix with a flat-bladed knife, using a cutting action, until a dough forms. Turn onto a floured surface and knead for 10 minutes, or until smooth. Transfer to an oiled bowl, cover with plastic wrap and leave for 45 minutes, or until doubled in size.

3   **Meanwhile, combine oil,** basil, garlic and prawns in a non-metallic bowl. Cover with plastic wrap and refrigerate for 30 minutes.

4   **Preheat the oven** to 230°C (450°F/Gas 8). Punch down the dough, then knead for 8 minutes, or until elastic. Divide into 24 balls. Roll each ball into a very thin circle 5 cm (2 inches) in diameter. Prick the surfaces with a fork and brush with oil.

5   **Place the bases** on a lightly greased baking tray. Spread ½ teaspoon of pesto over each base, leaving a narrow border. Put a prawn, basil leaf and pine nut on each pizza and bake for 8–10 minutes.

# TANDOORI CHICKEN MINI PIZZAS

**MAKES 24**

60 g (2 oz/¼ cup) ready-made tandoori paste

1 garlic clove, crushed

4 tablespoons chopped coriander (cilantro) leaves, plus extra for garnish

125 g (5 oz/½ cup) plain yoghurt

550 g (1 lb 4 oz) boneless, skinless chicken thighs, trimmed and cut into small dice

1 small cucumber, peeled, halved, seeds removed and chopped

1 tablespoon oil, plus extra for drizzling

2 teaspoons plain yoghurt, extra

24 pizza dough bases

**1   Combine the tandoori** paste, garlic, 3 tablespoons of the coriander, and 60 g (2 oz/¼ cup) yoghurt in a non-metallic bowl. Toss the chicken in the mixture, then cover and refrigerate.

**2   Meanwhile, put cucumber** in a sieve. Sprinkle with salt and leave for 30 minutes. Rinse, squeeze dry and combine with the remaining yoghurt and coriander. Refrigerate.

**3   Heat the oil** in a large frying pan and cook the chicken in batches over medium–high heat for 6–8 minutes, or until tender. Stir in the extra yoghurt. Spoon a heaped teaspoon of chicken on each base. Flatten with the back of the spoon. Drizzle with oil. Cook, then top with cucumber mix and garnish with coriander.

# MINI HAMBURGERS

**MAKES 24**

8 burger buns, split in half

400 g (14 oz) minced (ground) beef

25 g (1 oz/¼ cup) dry breadcrumbs

3 French shallots, very finely chopped

1 tablespoon dijon mustard

1 tablespoon worcestershire sauce

80 ml (3 fl oz/⅓ cup) tomato sauce

olive oil, for shallow-frying

100 g (4 oz) thinly sliced cheddar
cheese, cut into 24 squares, each
3 cm (1¼ in)

24 baby rocket (arugula) leaves, stems
removed and torn into pieces

12 cornichons (baby gherkins), cut into
thin slices

**1** **Stamp out rounds** from the burger buns using a 4 cm (1½ in) cutter; you should get 24 from the tops and 24 from the bases. If the buns are quite thick, trim them with a serrated knife after you have cut them.

**2** **Combine the mince,** breadcrumbs, chopped French shallots, mustard, worcestershire sauce, 1 tablespoon of the tomato sauce and some salt and cracked black pepper in a bowl. Divide the mixture into 24 walnut-sized pieces. With wet hands, shape the pieces into patties.

**3** **Heat a large** heavy-based frying pan with enough oil to just cover the bottom of the pan and cook the patties over medium heat for about 1 minute on each side, or until browned, then place on a baking tray.

**4** **Lightly grill both** halves of the mini burger buns. Top each patty with a small slice of cheese and grill for 1 minute, or until the cheese is just starting to melt.

**5** **Place the patties** on the bottom halves of the burger buns. Top with the rocket, cornichon and remaining tomato sauce. Gently press on the top half of the burger bun and secure with a cocktail stick. Serve warm.

# CHIPOLATA SAUSAGES WITH HORSERADISH CREAM

**MAKES 12**

| |
|---|
| 2 tablespoons olive oil |
| 2 red onions, cut into thin wedges |
| 2 tablespoons dark brown sugar |
| 3 teaspoons balsamic vinegar |
| 100 g (4 oz) cream cheese |
| 1 tablespoon horseradish cream |
| 12 chipolata sausages |
| 12 par-baked mini bread rolls |
| 100 g (4 oz) rocket (arugula) leaves, stalks removed |

**1**  Preheat the oven to 220°C (425°F/Gas 7). Heat about 1½ tablespoons olive oil in a small saucepan. Add onion and 1½ tablespoons water. Cover and cook over medium heat for about 10 minutes, stirring occasionally, until onion is soft and starting to brown. Stir in sugar and vinegar and cook, uncovered, for 3 minutes, or until thick. Season. Keep warm.

**2**  Meanwhile, combine the cream cheese and horseradish cream in a small bowl and mix until smooth.

**3**  Heat remaining oil in a large frying pan and cook the sausages in batches over medium–low heat for 6–8 minutes, or until brown and cooked. Remove and drain on crumpled paper towels.

**4**  Meanwhile, heat bread rolls according to manufacturer's instructions. When hot, slice horizontally, three-quarters of the way through, and spread with the horseradish mixture. Fill the rolls with rocket and a sausage, then onion. .

# INDEX

GREAT TASTES FINGERFOOD